The Left-Handed Curriculum

Creative Experiences for Empowering Teachers

The Left-Handed Curriculum

*Creative Experiences
for Empowering Teachers*

Morna McDermott

Towson University

INFORMATION AGE PUBLISHING, INC.
Charlotte, NC • www.infoagepub.com

Library of Congress Cataloging-in-Publication Data

A CIP record for this book is available from the Library of Congress

Library of Congress Control Number: 2012953966

Printed in the United States of America

Contents

PART **II**

Theory into Action

Acknowledgements

This book is dedicated to my father Jack McDermott, my mother Polly McDermott, my husband Leonard McNulty, and my two children Conor and Molly. These are the people who have been, and continue to be, my most significant teachers.

This book would not have been possible it were it not for two of my Lesley University mentors: Elijah Mirochnick and Gene Diaz. Their ongoing guidance and wisdom have inspired me, just as I know they have inspired scores of teachers and teacher educators everywhere. I would also like to extend my deepest appreciation to Karen Minette Weinstein for being a faithful and honest reader. Her insight shaped this book so much.

This book is written for, and emerges from, the individual and collective passions, insights, courage, and commitment of the teachers I have had the honor to work with, notable those teachers from all over the country who have been part of the Lesley University Creative Arts in Learning graduate program. Without them, this book would not have been possible. Ideas are only as good as their implementation. While I constructed the course readings and activities for my graduate level Lesley courses, it was the teachers who came—bringing their hopes, their experiences, their histories, their fears, and their imaginations—and took the risks to rediscover their profession and themselves that made what I hope is a meaningful approach to curriculum for others. The experiences outlined in this book grew organically from the feedback of these teachers, collected from my first year and growing each year after that. Each experience in this book was honed and perfected based on their feedback. This is their book.

Lastly, this book is dedicated to educators everywhere, in every setting; educators who continue to fight against forces that try to put teachers and students in little boxes or to destroy our most vital resource: our capacity to imagine. Together we remind ourselves of the old phrase: Never, never, never give up.

Foreword

Welcome to an exciting journey into the land of learning, a tour along the course of left-handed ideas that will stimulate your imagination and awaken your senses as you travel to the plains of possibilities. Along the way theory and action will entice you with their unique precision and agile capacity to dance together in a tantalizing tarantella of teaching. In the fields where the muses convene to craft the many artful ways they sing their songs of curiosity and wonder, fireflies will pulsate and glow around you with the many hues and tones of creativity. Sound too vividly colorful for teacher education? Learning, as McDermott so deftly describes, can really be this fun.

Yet taking this journey involves risk. Where we are going is unknown territory for many of us. The languages of the arts might be unfamiliar and strange to you, and a commitment to engage in the conversation will take courage and some amount of daring. Like traveling to a new culture, you might find yourself sometimes lost and frequently confused by the practices and norms others seem to know with ease. I encourage you to take the leap into the unknown and experience the spirit of learning, that opening up of yourself to the new bright sky of sometimes cloudy, sometimes pristine possibility. Experience again, as you did when you were young, the eye-opening wonder, laced with some trepidation, of feeling the earth move beneath your feet, of exploring a path that leads to somewhere you have never been.

McDermott accompanies us along that path only a short distance and then she pushes us forward, out on our own, to find that curriculum that

The Left Handed Curriculum, pages ix–xii
Copyright © 2013 by Information Age Publishing
All rights of reproduction in any form reserved.

is unknowable and unpredictable. Students need to see that more is possible . . . and that more possibilities exist for them to imagine. These possibilities possess real consequences since, as McDermott notes, "Critical aesthetics allows us to peer through a lens where justice and democratic ideals might be seen and heard from outside the mainstream authoritative paradigm of more traditional curricula." It for us, as educators, to open up new aesthetic vistas for our students, to move beyond the authoritative mainstream into the land of hope and justice.

Practicing theory through what she terms "teacher experiences," she outlines activities for building bubbles and constructing catapults, performing theatrical compositions, creating 2D and 3D collage structures, fabricating teacher dolls within boxes, and painting the future of the teaching profession. McDermott takes us to class with her through her detailed descriptions of the activities and the vivid examples of her students' work that illustrate their own learning and growth. This unique volume presents us with her ideas about creativity, curriculum, and art, as well as her deep understanding of the context in which teachers labor in this country.

She reminds us—no, she shows us—that curriculum is not an object we hold in our hands, but a process, an emergent, collaborative, and potentially transformative process. Yes, it is also the course that we run, walk, leap, and fly through down a path, along a journey. To make that journey meaningful for you and for your students, you must make it memorable. Aesthetically reconceived curriculum engages us all in a memorable experience. Aesthetic experience based in a fully wide-awake engagement with the sensual world around us will awake within a feeling, yes, *feeling* of the awesomeness of it all. That is something we will remember.

From Carey's framework of critical aesthetics and Gablik's ideas of a post avant-garde, McDermott creates for us a new heuristic, the "critical post avant-garde." Now that's really so far outside of our typical discourse in teacher education that we have to stretch to our conceptual limits, and then go beyond, to even get a glimpse of it. Stretching conceptually, similar to stretching our physical bodies, requires careful concentration to identify the places where our elasticity finds a limit, and then moving just beyond that place. Like our bodies, our minds tend toward rigidity over time; we stay within the comfortable, the known, the tested (yes, the tested) areas that have worked for us before. Without continuing to stretch, we will continue to tighten, to become less flexible and more rigid. This analogy between the mind and the body will break down at some point, but I challenge you to consider it and verify that your own ideas and muscles have become less flexible over time. Within these pages you will find new ways to stretch, leading to increased flexibility and vigor in your ideas about curriculum.

Yet you won't be taking this journey alone, exploring, stretching, and encountering the unknown. This work is done in concert, together with others. Each of the activities that you find in this book involves a collaborative effort in which students will be working together with each other and with you as facilitator. Take the risk and try them with your students. Experience collaborative learning that will surprise you with the creativity it generates in you and in your students. Those of us who have been on this path for many years welcome you to this side of the curriculum.

—**Gene Diaz**
Cambridge, MA

PART **I**

Introduction

While the phrase "teacher empowerment" has been documented for a few decades (Marks & Louis, 1999; Rice & Schneider, 1994), it has a new meaning in light of the recent "education reform" measures that use discrediting professional educators as part of the effort to "turn schools around." There has been a paradigm shift in the last two decades, growing increasingly more powerful, beginning with the advent of No Child Left Behind (NCLB) in the 1990s until present day with Race to the Top (RtTT) and the push for corporate-run public education "alternatives." This paradigm shift reflects an era of education reform that is driven by (among other things) high stakes testing and efforts by policy makers to make the curriculum "teacher proof." According to Taffee (2009):

> While no longer in vogue, the term "teacher-proof" was coined decades ago with the advent of direct instruction models of teaching such as *DISTAR* and *Open Court* to assure school administrators that no matter the background, creativity, skills, or knowledge of their faculty, the program would work as long as the teachers stuck to the script. The curriculum was fool-proof, even though (most) teachers are not fools. (n.p.)

I am reminded of the medicine bottles in my bathroom cabinet that are "child proof"—meaning that neither of my two children have access to the contents therein, no matter how badly they want to open them. In this same vein, today's efforts to "standardize" teaching and to "teacher-proof" the curriculum deny teachers a certain amount of needed autonomy over

The Left-Handed Curriculum, pages 3–11
Copyright © 2013 by Information Age Publishing
All rights of reproduction in any form reserved.

the curriculum that they are required to enact; a curriculum hoisted on them from "above," and by which their own abilities and skills in the profession will be evaluated. Such efforts have dire consequences for the future of public education. In a teacher-proof curriculum, teachers cannot (or are afraid to) modify instructional strategies or assessments in order to meet the needs of *their* unique students or classroom community. The primary goals of the one-size-fits-all model are to keep pace, stay on the calendar with the scripted expectations, and teach only what will be tested. This new paradigm inculcates teachers with the idea that curriculum developers (aka textbook and testing companies) know more about the methods and content of what should be taught than the teachers themselves who have personal relationships with the students they serve.

Furthermore, the punitive measures attaching curriculum directly to testing measures (see www.unitedoptout.com; www.fairtest.org) leaves teachers fearful of deviating from the proscribed mandates they must deliver. A student-centered curriculum implemented by empowered knowledgeable educators is now even farther beyond reach, and one that is creatively *enacted* by teachers *with* their students often seems impossible. What we have instead is a corporate-centered curriculum—one that suits the agenda of the test makers (who profit in billions of dollars with the forced implementation of new teacher and student evaluation systems), and online "alternative" for-profit educational service providers that are orchestrated by big business.

But there are always little inroads, ruptures, fissures, or cracks in any system. As Powell and Speiser (2004) remind us, there are "little signs of hope." My mischievous and clever son, much to my own chagrin, at the age of six has cracked the child-proof medicine bottle code. He has found a way to get into that bottle of fruity gummy vitamins at will. How? By trial and error, by watching me closely as I twist the bottle, by taking risks, experimenting, and not giving up (when I'm not looking). He has essentially used the basic elements of creative (dare I say artful) problem-solving. These same elements are what are needed now, to be embraced by educators, in order to take back the curriculum and bring creative and critical thinking back to the craft of their profession—and by doing so, share it in creative and collaboratively designed ways with their students.

This book distinguishes itself from other books written about creativity and art in education in that it focuses on the importance of creative thinking specific *to teachers themselves*. This book also focuses on creativity in teaching as a *collaborative* effort. Our 21st-century global society demands empathetic, imaginative, and innovative ways of being and becoming for both teachers and students that are focused on socially just local and global practices. One innovative approach toward social change is through arts-based or creative community-oriented and collaborative modes of activism (Richards & Haynes, 1996; Schwarzman & Knight, 2005).

While books abound for individuals on how to become more creative, and many are specifically focused on teachers (see Gilbert & Ryan, 2011; Tan, 2007; Tan & Lai-Chong, 2004), most texts are instructional and they focus on how teachers can inspire creative thinking for *their* students. Few resources are available about how to provoke small groups of educators or whole communities of educators to work together and support each other in *their own* creative efforts. In essence, if teachers are to inspire creative, arts-informed practices in their classrooms, they first must be allowed the opportunities to broaden their own creative horizons as practitioners. As the saying goes: You cannot give away something you haven't got. To begin this journey requires no capital "A" artistic skill sets. A teacher need not have any formal or informal artistic training.

What *is* needed to transform schools into democratic and sustainable sites of creative empowerment for students and teachers is *not* one more curriculum "guide," or codified and copyrighted terminology that simply repackages what most of us already know as good practice and common sense. What is needed simply is that we *re-perceive*, that we see differently, the qualities and facets of our educational practices that are already in existence, and that in doing so, we discover/uncover creative means for making the changes ourselves. What is needed most is courage. And faith—in ourselves, and in our students.

What this book proposes is a set of creative experiences to be performed by teachers, and each requires only the development of a broader set of aesthetic sensibilities that are best brought forward through arts-based and creative processes. These experiences require only the willingness to embrace some basic concepts: emergence, collaboration, and transformation. This book is vital to redirect the course that public education is currently taking, to re-empower educators as professionals, and to inspire democratic ethics of social justice and community building within public education.

The creative and artful thinking that teachers can develop through embracing the experiences proposed here inspires them with the creative and critical thinking skills that are fostered through seeing themselves and the world as emergent (not fixed), relational (collaborative, not isolated), and transformative (having the capacity to change). Each of these themes will be discussed more thoroughly throughout this book, both in theory and practice. But I will define each concept here briefly.

Emergence

Emergence may be understood as the process by which something comes into being, often associated with organic processes rather than with pre-planned, predictable, or forced events. Emergence comes from acts of spontaneity and the unknown, which break us free from preconceived forms and expectations. Emergence is associated with organic processes that cannot be premeditated or controlled like products in a machine. The experiences in the book, such as Building the Bubble, composition work, and *Paint Your Life*, guide teachers as participants through this process with surprising results.

Collaboration (or Relationality)

Relational ways of being, or collaboration, involve examining the multiple ways in which things, people, places, and events correspond to one another, both spatially and in temporality, the juxtapositions of which create multiple meanings through working together. In other words, the outcomes that emerge from in-between events, people, and things, affect—and are affected by—the interactive processes themselves. As an agent for creative change, collaboration becomes the way in which we "engage space through the collaboration of multiple participants who share various social concerns and interests" (Carpenter & Springgay, 2011, p. 97). In Chapter 2, *Building the Catapult, Building Community*, teachers renew their sense of community building with one another, taking fresh perspective on how collaboration might be achieved.

Transformation

A change that occurs from within, and in tandem to existing parameters or conditions, creates a shape-shifting between what is within the individual and what is external, thus affecting both the individual(s) and the environment around them. Such a process does not make something new, but alters existing materials (mental, physical, and/or spiritual) into alternative forms of becoming or being. In one of the most powerful experiences, *Self, Curriculum, and Collage* in Chapter 4, teachers draw upon both emergence and collaboration to transform both self and classroom through the creative process. The example of teacher-led social activism in Chapter 5 (Part II) calls on teachers to carry their "wide-awakeness" (Greene, 1995) into the public sphere where they are empowered to change educational policies.

In order to reimagine what public schools and classroom communities might look like, when inspired by creative forms of teacher empowerment, we must first reexamine what we mean by certain terms. The title of this book is *Left-handed Curriculum,* which gives a nod of honor to the text *Left-Handed Teaching* by Castillo-Feliu (1978) who, like me, posed the question: "What understandings, values, and commitments do we want to teach our children?" (p. 20). A "left-handed" approach to curriculum suggests that educators be inspired by and practiced in teaching that uses the creative right side of their brains.

In keeping with a "right-brained/left-handed" approach, I define the term *curriculum* more broadly than being a simple set of guides, steps, materials, and pre-formed assessments to be delivered in a classroom. From the right side of our brains, curriculum might encompass creative, emotional, and intuitive skill sets that have been sterilized out of teacher-proof curricula and that are erased by standardized testing. A broader understanding of curriculum will be explored in the next section of this book.

Most people think of the "arts" in education as something they do once a week in related arts classes, or that fun activity a teacher pulls out on a rainy Friday afternoon. But the importance of encouraging creativity and imagination through artful experiences goes well beyond Howard Gardner's (1999) application of Multiple Intelligences. While multiple intelligences, related arts, and "fun" in learning are all indeed valuable and worthy of our attention in education, something much more valuable is being lost in the race toward a standardized curriculum, accountability, and high stakes testing.

When I teach my students (both preservice teachers/undergraduate students and experienced teachers/graduate students) about the value of arts and creativity in education, I always ask them why they think they're important. The number one response is "The arts make learning fun." OK, sure, stating the obvious, like: gravity makes things fall. So I challenge them to think deeper. What else? They sometimes add, "The arts teach students to have aesthetic appreciation for high culture which includes the 'masterpieces' hung in famous galleries." OK...although this response avoids the problems of an educational practice itself fraught with complexities of race, class, and gender, as these factors often remain invisible when appreciating the "High Art classics."

But I push them further. I ask, "What about the role of arts in imagining and creating solutions to local community and global problems? What about the importance of art in naming peoples and experiences that otherwise would remain silenced or invisible?" To these questions I usually I get blank stares in return.

You see, as we remove the arts and the capacity to think imaginatively from our classrooms, policymakers can argue, "Learning can't be fun anymore. That's too trivial. We need to work. Our students are failing!" And as for the second role of the arts? You might hear the argument, "Learning about the high arts in museums is trivial in comparison to preparing them for a seat in the global marketplace. It's fluff." These two first premises make it easy to argue for the reduction or elimination of arts in learning.

But what about the third thing that art enables students to learn about? It is the loss of the third that makes me lie awake at night.

The imagination—our capacity to be creative (and equally innovative)—is central to identifying and solving the crisis we face in the world today. We will not find the solutions to ending problems like poverty, racism, war, or global climate change on a standardized test. We create these solutions in the worlds that do not yet exist. The solutions lie in our capacities to imagine, in the words of Maxine Greene (1995), "things as if they could be otherwise" (p. 54).

Naomi Wolf recently published a book and made a documentary on the book, both entitled *The End of America* (2007). She argues that there are ten things needed in order to create a closed society, one that is not supported by democratic beliefs and policies. I might suggest to her to add one more item to the list. Number 11 on the list of things needed in order to create a closed society would be: putting an end to public education that is creative, meaningful, and rich in the experiences it provides for everyone in the school community. You see, in order to close a society you have to close the minds of its people. As we erase our children's capacities to wonder, to question, to create, and to *imagine*, we close off their minds from the possibilities of seeing their world as anything other than the one that is being handed to them. In order to close a society one must have a people who are unable to challenge the decisions being made or to question those in power making the decisions. Saltmarsh (2007) contends that "the widespread retreat from participation and *direct experiences* tend to limit political action to a narrow definition of procedural democracy" (p. xix, emphasis added).

A one-size-fits-all model of curriculum and assessment attached to high-stakes testing and punitive measures (defined as standardized testing) enforces fear-based accountability practices. While one could argue it *might* teach students the basics of reading and math, it does little to encourage the meaningful application and analysis of the information being spoon-fed to the students.

We want schools where students, teachers, and communities are collaborators in their efforts to provide learning experiences that have meaning for students. I argue for a creative approach that embraces culturally relevant pedagogy (Robinson & Lewis, 2011); artful ways of being that bring marginalized voices and experiences back to the foreground of our curriculum and classrooms. We want schools to be places where children can *create* the world they wish to see, rather than simply be tested on the world as it is. As Weida (2011) illustrates: "It might be argued that teaching and art-making share qualities of hybridism, fluidity, and openness to many different kinds of practices and practitioners" (p. 148).

The elimination of the arts and imaginative thinking from every classroom will confirm or solidify our fate as people dependent on those in power (at the top) who historically profit at the expense of those beneath them. These are the same people to whom we will be completely reliant upon to make decisions for us. The capacity to critically challenge or imagine a "way out," created for ourselves by ourselves, will have been educated *out* of us.

The knowledge and ideas of students, teachers, and communities are being erased from the classroom in favor of a sterilized, technical, rigid, and homogenous approach to learning. We need to fight for creative and artistic educational experiences that encourage collaboration, community centeredness, intercultural exchanges, and diverse perspectives. Through creative and artistic engagements, new voices can be heard and the faces of cultures and communities rendered visible. The imagination not only entertains. It is a powerful means of making cracks and fissures in the massive wall of educational policies that see students merely as consumers of textbook knowledge—knowledge that is prescripted for them. The curricula are prescriptions delivered in medicine bottles with safety caps. Our children are not commodities to be mined, as Sir Ken Robinson once said, "the way that we mine the earth for a particular commodity" (2007). And education has become a commodity, through a process in which textbook companies and corporate billionaires use high-stakes testing as a way to profit from both the success and failure of children in public schools.

The arts, as a collaborative community-based effort to transform ourselves, are the most vital tool we have to create a sustainable revolution. *It's not what we know, but what we can imagine* that will save humanity from the self-imposed crisis we can no longer evade. In the words of Grace Lee Boggs (Boggs & Kurashige, 2011), "Students are crying out for another kind of education that gives them opportunities to exercise their creative energies because it values them as whole human being" (p. 145). She also argues that revolutions are made not to prove the correctness of ideas but to begin anew. In a certain sense, this work often feels like a voyage out, from the habitual, the customary, the taken for granted, toward the unfamiliar, the more spontaneous, the questionable. The experimental posture in its most profound meaning suggests we seek openness to what is not known, and a willingness to attempt action the consequences of which cannot be predicted fully. (Pinar, 1998, p. 349)

But such a "voyage out" must be taken together. This book embraces a reframing of the narrative around art and creativity as things performed and created together. As Goldbard (2006) states:

> [W]ithout collective experience of self discovery, without participatory learning about themselves as a group and about their community, without meaningful participation in shaping collaboratively created work, the project does not contribute directly to community cultural development. (p. 141)

What Goldbard suggests about creativity in community development I extend to the communities we call schools. This book proposes is a series of experiences, which aim at generating community-based creative empowerment for teachers and schools to re-envision their vocation and the future of their classrooms. We need to begin anew, and we must educate our children with the capacities to engage with their own humanity and with one another.

Art, Boggs and Kurashige (2011) suggest, can help us envision a new cultural image we need to grow our souls. I would add that we transform ourselves into agents of change through the artistic application of technique and aesthetic analysis of curriculum. The poet Charles Bukowski (1975) wrote that "to do a dangerous thing with style" (n.p.) is what he called "art." Education needs to become a dangerous thing done with style (a topic explored later in this book). More than an object of art, curriculum is a visceral map of our cultural and social landscapes, a metaphoric and literal representation of particular values and beliefs. As such, it is through the creative process that such values and beliefs might also be challenged and critically redefined. When we lose our imaginative capacities to envision and argue for social change and to face an unknown future, I indeed fear for the end of our democratic society. We cannot let that happen.

Origins of This Book

The ideas, data, and work samples documented in this book came from ten years of teaching a class called *Curriculum Theory, Design and Assessment (through the arts)*, taught as part of Lesley University's Creative Arts in Learning distance-learning graduate program. This program brings graduate courses to sites across the country in cohorts of teachers seeking to complete their graduate degree. I had the pleasure to work with teams of 10–25 teachers in each cohort across the country from Washington to Georgia. Taught as a "weekend intensive" class, on two weekends four weeks apart, we spent most of our hours going through the experiences outlined in this book. Building upon the assigned class readings and drawing from (and developing our own) theories and practices for left-handed teaching practices, we collaboratively developed ways to reclaim our profession and for them to share these experiences with their own students. Over the years, I have honed these creative experiences into a specific multilayered process grounded in the themes of *collaboration, emergence,* and *transformation.* The order in which each experience is presented in this book is very deliberate, as each one is layered upon (or spirals from) the one prior, building conceptual and creative awareness in the teacher-participants as they move through them.

Each chapter of the book in Part II contains a theory and a practice section. When you utter the word "curriculum" to many teachers, their eyes glaze over. Understandably so, I might add. But theoretical conceptions are not merely talk from the ivory tower. *Theory* (for living and/or for education) is something each of us lives every day, embedded in our perspectives, values, and beliefs. For example, are you a person who views the cup of life as half full or half empty? The answer to this question is a theory about life, and it shapes how one chooses to interact and make decisions. Whether teachers consciously recognize it or not, each of us also has our own theory of education. This theory is shaped by, and in turn shapes, how and what we teach. A *creative* theoretical (re)framing is vital for educators to be fully cognizant of *how* the experience in each chapter developed, its larger purpose, and *why* it is important to altering the current education landscape.

Education has increasingly become less of a profession and more of a "task," one that simply demands blind compliance on behalf of teachers who are not given opportunity to understand whose values or motives are behind pedagogical decisions, but to "do it" simply because they're "told to do so." Theories may clash, collide, and differ. There is no one right theory for education. But the experiences I propose are squarely and deliberately set within education theories, which will be discussed further in Part I.

I owe each and every teacher that I worked with a debt of gratitude, not only for allowing me to share their experiences so that I could write this book, but for the volumes of courage and wisdom they have offered, thus transforming my own educational theory and practice in ways I never could have imagined alone.

Defining Aesthetics, Art, Creativity, and Curriculum

Creative solidarity is the necessary act of forward motion, in a collective movement.
At this precise moment in our history it demands of us that we search for new
and emerging structures of feeling, for languages and ideas for doing our work,
for new ways of being with each other, for ways of forging new trails,
leaving new footprints, new ripples in our wake.
—(Gatzambide-Fernandez, 2010, p. 91)

Aesthetics, art, creativity, and *curriculum* are the most frequently used terms in this book. Before immersing oneself in the experiences proposed in Part II, the reader must first consider how the central terms—*aesthetics, art, creativity* and *curriculum*—are being defined and applied. Therefore, the first section of this book is dedicated to (re)defining each of these terms as they will be used in the ensuing chapters and embodied within each of the experiences. The reader should take this recontextualizing of the terms into his or her personal and individualized understanding as each is applied to the experiences discussed in Part II: Chapters 1–6.

Aesthetics: Not Just for Drinkers of Fancy Wine

When discussing the term "art," the concept of aesthetics cannot be evaded. Aesthetics is a word usually associated with museum curators, arts historians, and people who hang out in high-rent metropolitan apartments sipping expensive wine and discussing matters that most educators could care less about. So before we move forward, it's important to set the record straight. Aesthetics, in laymen's terms for people like you and me, simply refers to the balance of sensory inputs we perceive from the qualities of light, color, texture, sound, movement, and so on from a particular object or set of surroundings. This is the aesthetics of everyday living. Stop for a moment. Pick your head up from his book and look around: What do you see? What do you smell? What do you hear? How do you feel in relationship to what you perceive right now? Is the space crowded and noisy? Still and silent? Open or cramped? Is the light bright or dim? How are things arranged? What mood do these arrangements elicit in you?

When working with teachers and leading them through the experiences outlined in this book, I begin by presenting different works of art in extreme contrast with each other to prompt the teachers to think of how the aesthetic arrangement of a painting shares certain aesthetic qualities with their own classrooms. For example: which of these works of art better resembles your classroom on a given day?

Artwork by Thaneena McArdle   Artist Unknown

While both are colorful, a word most teachers would use to describe their classrooms (as all children indeed have "colorful personalities," and we like to make learning exciting and "colorful"), notice the difference in how the lines *move*, the ways the colors are blended (or not), or the emotions each painting might elicit. Does the one on the left feel powerful and exciting, or just intimidating? Does the one on the right appear playful and more welcoming, or just chaotic? Teachers can discover a lot about who they are when they apply these aesthetic concepts to the movement, organization (or chaos), sounds, and interactions within their classrooms. How does the arrangement of these different qualities of sound, movement, and color affect what our students do, and how they do it? If we rearrange the various aesthetic pieces, will the very purposes and outcomes of our teacher–student interactions be transformed?

Art and Creativity as Relational Concepts

Art is rarely (if ever) automatically "transformative" by itself. In fact, sometimes it is used to re-entrench dominant worldviews and narratives (see Anderson, 2011). As Goldbard (2006) points out, a "painting has never possessed the power to move political worlds" (p. 14). It is what *we do* with art that matters. Additionally, creativity is not inherently a liberatory process and is often associated exclusively with children identified as gifted or otherwise privileged. And curriculum, as it is practiced in most K–12 settings, is most often confining and limiting in its definition and scope. As I have expressed in previous scholarship (McDermott, 2001):

> The use of aesthetics and art by themselves do not automatically lead towards "liberation" from taken-for-granted and potentially exclusionary practices. For instance, because "a dominant narrative," according to Gablik (1995), is reproduced as a universal and "race-free" narrative, it invisibly impresses upon "Other" cultures fixed values that determine social constructions of truth and meaning through language. Under the pretense of being progressive and "universal," dominant Western values of art and schooling entrap our subjective experiences "by other kinds of logic, or regimens, that are more subtly introduced into the subjects own mind through modern society" (Shusterman in Gablik, 1995, p. 7). (p. 183)

What makes art transformative hinges on who is creating it, the context in which it is created, and its purpose.

Creativity is often cited as the luxury of gifted children and curricula, or relegated to the insular world of "artists" (defined narrowly by societal terms of High Art). While creativity and arts-based educational practices are not synonymous, I use both in tandem (though not interchangeably) with one another, and therefore discuss both in the same section using the same framework. The possible relationships between aesthetics and art, as each relates to curriculum, will be revisited in the section called "Broadening Our Understanding of What Curriculum 'Is'." However, reconceiving of curriculum involves a reconception of what is meant by art and creativity as well.

Reexamining and Redefining Art and Creativity through Critical Post-Avant-Garde Aesthetics

Both terms—art and creativity—are commonly coopted by modernist or Westernized epistemologies, becoming products defined as individualized, for the elite, or reserved for what Carpenter and Springgay (2011) call "the creative class" (p. 97). One need simply look at the demographics of children in Western society defined by schools as creatively "gifted" according to race and social class to see how privilege shapes our expectations. Art programs are continuously cut from lower-income school communities, yet provided in spades to affluent schools, a systemic problem that highlights the roles that race and social class play in defining who can participate in "the arts." Additionally, in school art curricula, we celebrate male Caucasian Western (including United States and Western European) artists as the "masters" to be studied while rendering invisible the works of women and people of color whose works of art are embedded within deeper issues of community and social justice.

Generally speaking, creativity can be defined as the production of both novel and appropriate work (see Lubart, 2000; Sternberg & Lubart, 1996). Something novel is akin to something original that has no precedent and could not be anticipated nor predicted (see my discussion on emergence). Western assumptions about creativity include a "linear movement toward a new point" (Starko, 2010, p. 22)—a trajectory outward and away from existing origins (ironically the opposite of the meaning of "original"). These were the hallmark qualities of "modern" art of the early 20th century: detached from societal concerns, performed by lone artists, creating "art for art's sake."

Conversely, Starko explains that "Csikszentmihaly saw creativity not as a characteristic of particular people or products but as an interaction among person, product, and environment. The person produces some variation in the information gained from the culture in which he or she lives" (p. 60). Creativity does not just exist for individuals in isolated contemplation. It does not merely include work that is severed from what is old in favor of something new. Creativity resides in the relational work that community members forge together toward a shared vision, one that must reconceive both *how* we move forward in relationship to one another, and where we are going.

In keeping with a more relational view of creativity, many of the experiences described in this book require group or collaborative efforts. The results of structuring each activity in this way are that teachers break away from the isolation they feel on a daily basis when trying to become more creative on their own, and the isolation many feel within their classrooms.

To engage with something artistically usually demands our creative resources. Yet, this is not always the case. Jardine, Graham, LaGrange and Kisling-Saunders (2006) remind us that having children simply color in photocopied art worksheets (while technically defined as an arts-based activity) is very limited in culling children's imaginative capacities. There is little or no innovative or out-of-the-box thinking required in order to "color within the lines" (p. 229). Such definitive one-size-fits-all "creative" activities reinforce the idea that "lines" of conformity are everywhere in children's (*and teachers'*) lives—straight and linear, with distinct boundaries and rules of correctness in their supposed self-expression. Jardine et al. (2006) argue that:

> Instead of keeping children "together" within the bounds of the abstract black-lines...children can be kept "together" within the more sensuous, more ambiguous, more tangled, more rich, more compelling, more variegated, more demanding, more disciplined lines of a particular, located, encultured, historical, image-filled, worldly inheritance. (p. 331)

I believe that when creativity and art are seen from a more critical and collaborative perspective, they represent the creation of socially constructed knowledge and meaning making, where art can help transform schools and society. Gablik (1997) coined this kind of art movement as "post avant-garde." According to Gablik (1997), avant-garde art was the product of the Western modernist epistemologies of its era. In this context (like the modernist curriculum discussed in the next section of this chapter), art was perceived through a "disinterested, distanced, formal contemplation of the world" (p. 246). Further, she contests that such views of art reveal a "hidden elitism" in which "only certain people can take [such a view] . . . people whose practical world is already taken care of" (p. 248). This is what she calls the "museum conception of art" (p. 248). Museum conceptions of art, not unlike a modernist (or factory model) learning framework, reinforce the view that "the observer (is) a passive receiver, essentially Locke's blank slate, rather than as an active agent with a role to play in the construction of aesthetic experience" (Carey, 1998, p. 291).

Gablik's notion of *post*-avant-garde redefines art, "in the practice of living, in how we organize our lives and how we improve them, that the idea of confining art to what we hang on walls is a pathetic failure of theoretical as well as artistic imagination" (1991, p. 265). Post-avant-garde style embraces spontaneous creation and synchronous engagements between the self, art, and social context in which each is embedded. Gablik contends that rather than viewing the post-avant-garde as a fully realized framework, we might consider it more as a way to "think about new connections, participatory aesthetics, and to speak for a value-based art that is able to transcend the modernist opposition between the aesthetic and the social" (1997, p. 9).

Another key feature of post avant-garde art is that, as opposed to the modernist perception of the individual artistic genius working alone, art is a socially constructed act. It also subverts the notion that any form of art can be considered "new" or "ahead of its time," favoring instead the idea that, "art constructs the reality that is perceived . . . and offers multiple interpretations . . . each imbued with politics and ethics" (jagodinski, 1997, p. 143). Rather than searching for new "discoveries" (Gablik, 1997) the post avant-garde seeks out previously unacknowledged *relationships*. Richard Shusterman, in his interview with Gablik (1997), explains, "We are all recycling, quoting and appropriating" (p. 255), despite the strong emphasis we still place on the ideal of "pure innovation"(p. 255). Art becomes a vehicle for social awareness and collaborative action that lives in and through us— working with what we have, who we are, and where we wish to go.

Carey (1998) echoes the ideals expressed in the post-avant-garde in his exploration of critical aesthetics. He too argues for moving away from the traditional "values and tastes complicit with the interests of the powerful and the dominant" (p. 314) toward a praxis that "opens the knowledge process to the subjective qualities of lived experience that expand meaning beyond the reified, objective, decontextualized, pseudo-values predetermined and handed down by experts as the uncontested criteria for reality and truth" (p. 310).

When we embrace the potential for critical aesthetics to become central to a post-avant-garde framework, we inspire the development of socially constructed knowledge(s) and meaning-making, where art can help transform schools and society. Aesthetically based educational practices, embodied in creative thinking and arts-based experiences, signify "the possibility to transition into another mode of being—the freedom to change situations, to abolish a petrified, or blocked systems of conditioning" (Gablik, 1991, p.43). Using critical aesthetics, we can peer through a lens where justice and democratic ideals might be seen and heard from outside the mainstream authoritative paradigm of more traditional curricula. In other words, if "art has played a key role in forming our society's definition of reality" then it also "has the power to redefine that concept" (Gablik, 1991, p. 28).

The theory and activities in this book blend together Carey's framework of critical aesthetics and Gablik's notion of post-avant-garde, bringing both together into a heuristic I call "*critical post-avant-garde*" (CPAG) arts-based practices (McDermott, 2001). Critical post-avant-garde arts-based experiences infuse Gablik's post-avant-garde approach to art with a curricular "style" that analyzes aesthetics through a *critical* lens, transforming both method and ends of teaching in order to address educational issues in ways that might otherwise remain unseen or unheard. Ultimately, the method *is* the message.

Broadening Our Understanding of What Curriculum "Is"

> The point of curriculum study can be conceived of as a search for vision, for revelation that is original, unique, and that opens the knowing and appreciative eye to worlds hitherto unseen and unknown. (Pinar, 1998, p. 246)

Let's Do the Time Warp: Modern versus Postmodern Worldviews

To illustrate the relationships between art, life, and curriculum, I begin with a narrative as analogy:

> An artist, a woman and a gridded screen...the artist has set [the gridded screen] between himself and the nude [woman], so he can accurately plot her measurements and proportions. So rigidly preoccupied is the artist with the grid, that on the paper before him is no woman at all, no knowing smile, no thigh and no moist finger, just straight lines on the page, the frets of a grid. (Griffiths, 2004, p. 1)

Keeping this analogy in mind, I pose the question to teachers: *Do we teach a curriculum? Or, do we teach students?* As Griffiths illustrates in the narrative above, I similarly worry that "we are so preoccupied with our gridded, subdivided constructions of numbered measurements that we lose sight of the gorgeous, lifeful thing itself" (2004, p. 1). Such is the legacy of a modernist framework for education.

Just as Gablik and other artists have made the distinction between modern and postmodern art (and post-avant-garde as an emerging thread *within* postmodern conceptions of art), so too are there modernist or postmodern conceptions of curriculum. What happens when we blend together broadened perspectives of what art, creativity, and aesthetics are, with broader perspectives on what curriculum is, or *could* be? Curriculum is a term not unlike aesthetics in that it too is narrowly defined, and is left to ivory tower conversations among academics and policymakers. But, like the *real* everyday understanding of aesthetics, curriculum too is a simple and misunderstood term.

Teachers should be a vital part of discussions around curricular matters. But teachers must also be cognizant of larger theoretical frameworks for constructing curriculum in order to make critical and informed decisions. Here's a solid definition of curriculum—and it does not require you to whip out your thesaurus: *In its real and everyday context, curriculum is everything a child experiences from the moment he or she wakes up in the morning until the moment at which he or she goes to bed at night.*

The term used to describe a traditional (i.e., Western conception of) curriculum and model of schooling, one which reflects the societal moment in which it was created, is also called a "modernist" approach. Another word to describe this framework is a factory model since modern schools emerged during the Industrial Revolution and were modeled after that image. In fact, one need only look at existing curricula, in which instructional time is pinned down to the nearest minute, to see how this framework reflects a factory model of time. Griffiths (2004) points out that "minutes...were little used until the Industrial Revolution, which 'needed' more exact time measurement" (p. 2).

However, the scientific, social, political, and economic changes revolving around World War II had a ripple effect in changing our world in the decades that followed. Of particular note is the introduction of quantum physics, developed most notably by Albert Einstein. I won't even attempt to explain what that means here, but suffice it to say that our older Western assumptions about how the world worked (on an atomic level) described by Newton a century before in Newtonian physics—in which everything moves together in a predictable billiard-ball-like set of cause-and-effect relationships—was radically displaced with one that depicts the universe as a more chaotic and fluid place.

Interestingly enough, our sense of humanity was also moving from one where everything seemed fixed, and the "Truth" seemed self-evident, was being smashed. Security was replaced with uncertainty with the invention of the atomic bomb. The rise of Hitler and pursuant acts of genocide left us questioning our own "humanness."

On the heels of this, the United States confronted itself during the 1950s and 1960s where social unrest manifested in challenges to the Vietnam War, legalized racism, and rampant sexism. Everything we thought was so neat, linear, and predictable about our own identities was being turned on its head. Enter the postmodern era: fluid, unpredictable, emergent, and full of questions and fewer answers. And yet as our society has been changing, many of our assumptions about school, teaching, and learning have remained "stuck" in a modernist framework.

I tell teachers to think of postmodernism using the film *Pulp Fiction* (1994) as a prime example. In this film the first few frames present the end of the storyline, then it jumps to a few snippets of the beginning of the storyline, moves to the middle, and then returns to the ending. Time, space, and character overlap in multiple ways, and the audience must construct the meaning as the film moves along. This is vastly different than ("modern") films made in prior decades, with a unified and linear storyline, one that was predictable in plot and in which characters had fixed and unchanging identities. The bad guys always wore black hats. The good guys would always win. And the distinction between the two was always clear.

In this postmodern era in which students cry out for agency and relevancy within their schooling experience, we continue to entrench learning in fixed, unified, and linear conscriptions tied to a fixed common curriculum that is tethered to a disembodied, "objective" set of facts on standardized tests. The stylistic construction of curriculum as a modernist or technical framework leads to a presentation of knowledge as "static images," which we try to preserve in some "rational" state rather than the complex and ever-changing combination of experiences which make up our human condition. Nor does this approach take into consideration the possible ways in which this interchange may mutually shape both the function of curriculum, and the individuals engaged in the activities.

Curriculum, for each of us, includes (but is not limited to): how we move, what we know, whom we interact with, where we learn, what we learn, and who serves as our teachers. Curriculum includes our individual and shared lived contexts: (1) the historical moment (i.e., living in 2012 is different than or the same as living in 1942); (2) location (i.e., United States as opposed to China, Australia, or Russia; or northeastern U.S. versus the southern U.S.; urban versus rural); and (3) cultural contexts, which include but may not be limited to racial identity, religion, immigration status, and socioeconomic class. The list could be continued ad infinitum, but suffice it to say that curriculum is *always* more than what's written in the curriculum guide, what's printed on the worksheet, and what will be on the next test. It's more than the goals and objectives teachers write on the board. It's more than the materials needed to teach and learn. While these are all pieces of curriculum, they are not its sum total. Developing and practicing curriculum involves the various arrangements of these pieces listed above.

As with the discussion of aesthetics in art earlier in this chapter, there exists an aesthetics of curriculum. In curriculum development and practice, *what* is to be arranged, and *how* they are to be arranged matter greatly. A modernist (think: 1950s-era American) classroom curriculum, if reduced in an artist's sketch to mere lines, dots and colors, might look like this:

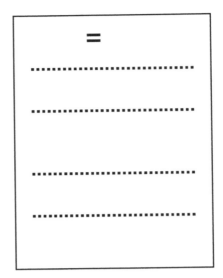

Lines and dots of modernity.

Why? The = represents the teacher and teacher's desk at the front. The dots/dashes represent the students at individual desks, all focused on the top of the image (or the front of the room). The image feels static and fixed. The curriculum is also static and fixed. It also eerily resembles both a worksheet and a bubble-dot standardized test. Form of learning and content of learning always directly interact with one another. Both are integral parts of what we call curriculum. Indeed this is so if we consider the kind of curricula that are delivered in classrooms that look like this: Knowledge is "delivered" in a very linear format (i.e., "We must do A before we can do B"), and subjects are treated in isolation from one another.

The image is in black and white, suggesting a few truths about modern day 1950s-style American public schools. First, until *Brown v. Board of Education* (1954), schools were (legally) racially segregated. Additionally, we have in our Western society since the advent of industrialization (the time period in which modern school were created, and hence in the "factory" image) this notion that "knowledge = facts," which are supposedly black and white, either right or wrong. We also presuppose in this modernist era of knowledge construction and meaning making that efficiency is of the highest value, and the assumption that learning takes place for each person in isolation at his or her desk seated in front of a textbook or worksheet.

But what if curriculum looked like this?

Pastel on paper, by Lori K, 2010.

If we were comparing the first image to this one, as works of art, we would be required to look at the aesthetics of both as part of our consideration. How do the lines, dots, and directionality of the image influence words we would use to describe each? And which do we prefer as a framework for creating our curriculum?

Curriculum as an Aesthetic (Postmodern) Text

In keeping with a modernist Western view of the world as linear and comprised of fixed Cartesian dualities (refer back to the first image on page 28 for a visual representation), "curriculum has been described using words such as: rational, implementation, evaluation, and as content to be studied; as a textbook; as a series of courses; or as a set of planned experiences" (Cornelius, 1999, p. 30). Curriculum, as a socially constructed phenomenon, is a Western notion of "time keeping" that is defined by "standardization and globalization" (Griffiths, 2004, p. 20).

Also evident in common assumptions of curriculum is the idea that knowledge moves in one direction, from instructor to learner, rather than in a more reciprocal or circular style, which might express exchange and mutual shaping between all of the respective "parts" (Freire, 1970/2000, 1998). The design and structure of a "modernist" standardized model for learning during the 20th century (and now into the 21st) embodies "underlying assumptions" about our Western ideologies reflected in the style of education. Levy (1996) contends, "The education industry...produces an endless supply of textbooks, teaching materials, learning kits, and lesson plans that define subject content. As such they organize information, package it for presentation, and provide practice drills and tests to determine if the children 'get it'" (p. 19).

As a result, "the entire world, it seems, has been rigorously processed and packaged for student consumption" (Levy, 1996, p. 19). Since the advent of No Child Left Behind and more recently, Race to the Top, textbook companies like Pearson and McGraw-Hill have made billions of dollars off of their testing and textbook relationships with public education.

The style of presenting knowledge as a discrete series of "facts" which can be learned and reproduced en mass, is a technique fashioned after and for an industrial society. The historically predominant design for learning as a linear sequencing of materials and objectives creates a style for knowledge production that is static and unchanging. Greene (1995) describes this style of schooling as being "preoccupied with test scores, 'time on task,' management procedures, ethnic and racial percentages, and accountability measures, while it screens out the faces and gestures of individuals, of actual living persons" (p. 11).

The traditional rational definition of curriculum, framed by Ralph Tyler (1949), developed during the midst of the industrial era and defined by technical and linear, objectified and absolute qualities, should give way to a more fluid and dynamic co-creation of form and substance. While a Tylerian model embodies a modernist approach, this book take a more postmodern approach; one rooted in creative, aesthetic, emergent, and critical qualities of what is known (or better yet unknown), by whom, how, and why. In contrast to a modernist Western concept of curriculum as a linear and fixed body of knowledge to be transferred from point A to point B, Carey (1998) illustrates that looking at curriculum through a critical aesthetic postmodern lens enables us to reexamine the methods and aims of education and to consider how knowledge is constructed, and to what ends. He writes, "Postmodern thought...recommends a suspicion of the arrogance inherent in regarding truth claims as objective and timeless. [It] also questions the implications for and tacit associations of such truth claims with various potentially oppressive power structures that influence human experience" (p. 7).

A more fluid postmodern framework of curriculum leads us towards kaleidoscopic and relational forms of knowing and being. Like the myriad of dynamic relationships between knower and known, "postmodern art reveals an abiding impulse to challenge power and authority in all forms" (Carey, 1998, p. 339). I parallel this definition of art to curriculum in that both might "contest exclusionary versions of reality and truth claims as final and ultimate" (p. 339). Diamond and Mullen (1999) write that in "venturing further into postmodernism," they "welcome the anxiety of leaving uncertainties and conflicts unresolved, and some questions unanswered" (p. 124).

What we do, how we perceive, and ultimately how we live, all require some employment of style. Style is how something is done. And the process (style) shapes the end results. Through creative efforts, curriculum might become a collaged style of teaching and learning. The gathering of relics from our contemporary lives, cultural mediums, and contexts are "cut" from experience and "pasted" onto our conscious mental, emotional, and mental frameworks into rearrangements: a collage of recreated moments transformed into perceptual reality. If, as Greene (1995) writes, "the form of representation feeds the life of meaning" (p. 96), then style and artistic representation become the outward expressions of this postmodern approach.

Curriculum from a postmodern perspective in part provides an aesthetic examination of what shall be cut, what shall be left out; it informs us about what is of value through presentation of materials and provides ways in which those cultural materials (i.e., assessments, texts, computers, content areas etc.) shall be arranged. In designing a curriculum, we might ask: who is the creator, who is it designed for, and to what end? Curriculum can "simply reinforce general conformity" (Carey, 1998, p. 60). However, looking at curricula and aesthetics through a critical postmodern lens (Carey, 1998) replaces the traditional concept of an aesthetic experience as a "heightened experience evoked by objective qualities with a concept of aesthetic experience as a consciously constructed cognitive reality that pervades lived experience and is manifested as social justice, peace and freedom from poverty, political systems' oppression, and so forth" (p. 304).

In a broader definition, left-handed curriculum can be understood as a style of arranged elements and actions built upon a specific structural design that shapes, and is shaped by, its context, resulting in a particular perception of reality (re)presented through knowledge and experience. Style shapes both what shall be included and what shall be left out of any given product or experience.

Refer back to the paintings on page 14. Each artist has a clear and distinct style, just as each teacher has his or her own style, or way of arranging aesthetic qualities within his or her classroom. Our curricula emerge from how we pace activities, how we arrange students to interact with one another, whether or not we embrace the "noisy classroom" or prefer quiet calm workspaces. Do we overlap and blend the content of lessons, or do we prefer to keep subjects clearly separated and neatly arranged? Each of the questions leads us to consider our own style of curriculum.

To that end, curriculum may be considered an "aesthetic text" (Pinar, 1995) through which we employ visual or aesthetic forms of literacy in order to structure meaning. Our educational practices are avenues towards desired ends, designed and implemented with the aim of manipulating the perception and experiences by which we construct society and ourselves. Such an approach moves our understanding of curriculum from a modernist (technical and linear factory) framing to one that is more postmodern (emergent, contextual, and layered).

Grumet (1978) argues that although curriculum may be examined from an aesthetic perspective, her definition suggests also that curriculum is not simply an artistic text. The artistic elements inherent in the creation and enactment of formal education are signifiers of more than the expressive intent of an artist. She distills three major ideas to make this illustration:

1. Curriculum is an aesthetic as well as a technological product, belonging to both the cultural and natural order. As a product of aesthetic activity it creates and encompasses both figure and ground. Figure is what we make prominent or important, while what is ground is what remains in the background. For example, what appears as figure in today's standardized curriculum? What will be on the test, or what is meaningful to the learners?

2. Curriculum, by providing a new gestalt[1] (the essence or shape of an entity's complete form), stands out against the ground of daily experience, both revealing and transforming it. As such, the making and performing of curriculum are both ongoing and incomplete processes. For example, how are all of the parts of a curriculum assembled to create a sense of the "whole" of the teaching and learning process?

3. Curriculum, once presented, tends to sink into the ground of daily experience, to mingle with it, and become confused with the natural order. This aesthetic critique requires that we "acknowledge that curriculum is the world of meanings that we have devised and that as teachers and students we assume responsibility for and for the action it admits" (Grumet, 1978, p. 286).

The creation of knowledge becomes a continuous thread of construction and reconstruction throughout our lives. If we consider curriculum as a device for structuring meaning, its intent may be revealed through the aesthetic relationship between the various parts. For example, how does a lesson change when it is structured as a group activity grounded in student-led problem solving as opposed to a teacher-led lesson presented at a chalkboard and concludes with a work sheet? What happens if we allow students to create pictures and songs to show understanding instead of writing a standard essay? In each example, the various parts of the curriculum are arranged differently and produce a different effect.

Slattery (1999) reflects that he "along with Dewey [believes that] education must enhance the lives of those who are marginalized and create social consequences of value" (p. 203). The role of aesthetic analysis and artistic production in education in this critical postmodern sense is to "offer an opportunity for multiple cultural art forms to inform the thinking process, evoke understanding, arouse passions, and inspire 'social consequences of value'" (Dewey, 1934, in Slattery, 1999, p. 205).

In discussing the importance of finding one's voice in education, we must consider that the position of teacher as active agent and student as passive recipient only reinforces the idea that the curriculum is a technical tool and the student is a subject to be acted upon. We might conclude as well, then, that now teachers are also considered subjects to be acted upon by corporate interests that are shaping the narrative of education reform. Curriculum design shapes students and educators thinking about their own sense of agency and identity within the classroom. Within these correspondences, the aesthetic representation of knowledge in a curriculum discloses "meaning" through "design of selections" (Pinar & Grumet, 1978, p. 319). Like the artist, material, and end product, the learning process should evolve as reciprocal and shifting events influenced by aesthetic properties arranged within a series of correspondences between the three agents: content, teacher, and student.

Pinar and Grumet (1978) believe that an "aesthetic critique of curriculum" might ideally "lead to a transformation in the way that situation is experienced" (p. 286). They continue, "Curriculum comes to form as art does, as a complex mediation and reconstruction of experience" (p. 286).

As mentioned in my introduction, the poet Charles Bukowski (1975) suggests, "To do a dull thing with style/Is preferable to doing a dangerous thing/Without it/To do a dangerous thing with style/Is what I call art" (n.p.). An aesthetic critique of curriculum design might either lead to the conclusion that curriculum is a "dull or static thing," or rather it might lead to a reconceptualization of learning that inspires a vision for change. I envision curriculum as an active arrangement of style and meaning, a dangerous thing that may be defined as art.

The Aesthetics of Curriculum as Dangerous Style

Style and form are the constructs of all creative efforts. Nothing can be done or completed without them. Taking Bukowski's words to heart, style might become an articulation of curriculum: meaning-making about the self and the world around us. We employ style in order to align, associate, and express. Style becomes a framework for what information might be revealed or constructed, and how that information is transformed into knowledge and understanding. Style, as Bukowski's poem suggests, lends itself to doing a "dangerous thing."

Carey (1998), in his discussion of art as a form of critical pedagogy, defines "style" in educational praxis as being similar to "style" in art in that, "styles of both art production and knowledge production amount to perspectives or tendencies toward action or dialogue instead of prescribed steps to follow" (p. 184). Curriculum as dangerous "style" might "assume different meanings at different times" (p. 184). If doing something dangerous with style is art, and if, as Carey argues, "education values one form of knowledge over others in education, and the difference creates and supports a hierarchy" (p. 4), then dangerous style might also elicit "dangerous memories" (p. 6) to shatter such hierarchies. Reflecting on the power of art and memory Carey (1998) writes:

> A dangerous memory—recall that Henry Giroux coined the expression—is the critical awareness of the historical roots of a discipline, including all the implicit and explicit influences that shaped current conditions. This form of memory often establishes the rationale for a radical re-conceptualization of education and a new visualization of its possibilities for the future. (p. 63)

Schools, like other cultural sites such as museums and art galleries, can become places to display artifacts of dominant cultural ideologies and "agents of social reproduction" (Carey, 1998, p. 51). On the other hand, using Carey's (1999) lens of critical aesthetic analysis, classrooms might also become sites that lead to "reveal unnoticed truths through creative expression, self-reflection, and cultural connections...providing the motivation and means to resist oppressive forces" (p. 65).

From a postmodern perspective, the aesthetics of language, vision, memory, desire, place, and placement continuously recombine themselves in our experiences, shaping the human experience while being simultaneously shaped by our manipulation of it. What the latest push for National Common Core State Standards (NCCS) attached to high-stakes testing and a continued practice of a Tylerian (modernist) model ignore in the educational landscape is that the "spaces" of an individual shape knowledge into "artifacts" of economic, historical, cultural, and autobiographical origins. These spaces require us to consider that "what counts as knowledge, of course, necessarily begins with knowledge of who the subject thinks she is" (Sumara & Davis, 1998, p. 4). If knowledge is individually and socially constructed, contingent upon who a person is and where they are (historically and geographically for example), then how can anything be "common" or absolute about how they construct meaning? How can such real learning be measured in absolute or fixed terms?

Handy Reference Chart of Concepts and Terms Comparing Modern and Postmodern Frameworks (within American/Western European societies)

Modern (aka Traditional)	Postmodern
From Renaissance to circa 1950	From circa 1950–present
Presumed dominance/superiority of Western European and American cultural values and practices	Challenges to Western European and American idealism. A more global and multicultural worldview emerges
Time and space are viewed as "machine-like": linear, unified, absolute, predictable, organized	Time and space are viewed as more "chaotic": unpredictable, overlapping, organic, fluid, relative, and emergent.
Key philosophies include Descartes and Newton	Key philosophies include Einstein's quantum physics and theory of relativity
Related historical events: Birth of the Renaissance, Western imperialism and colonialism, The Industrial Revolution, Age of "discovery."	Related historical events: World War I and II, the atomic bomb, the Civil Rights movement, U.S./Vietnam anti-war protest, Waning U.S. industrial power, Birth of the technological revolution, Globalization.
Curriculum as a social construction: Racially segregated, Curriculum as factory-model, "Scientifically driven" instruction, Ralph Tyler's model of goals and objectives, Learning as measurable and predictable, Students as empty vessels, Instructional design based on discrete subjects and linear presentation.	Curriculum as a social construction: Desegregation (at least legally) promotes new multicultural frameworks, Curriculum as aesthetic text, Knowledge is relational and socially embedded, Learning is fluid and dynamic, curriculum is interdisciplinary, Everything is related to everything else in overlapping and complex ways, Learning cannot be measured by predicable and absolute measurement and outcomes, curriculum .
Visual image:  (image courtesy of MS Word clip art)	Visual image: 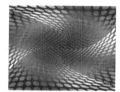 (image courtesy of MS Word clip art)

In the modernist and so-called objective world of education, students and teachers are like the realist painters separating the "I" in the eye of their work, reconstructing images with absolute realism, depicting the "true" nature of the object as if it were removed from any relationship with the artist.

In education, the "I" is how we see ourselves and the "eye" is how we perceive the world and our relationship to it. The modernist process of teaching creates a technical perspective similar to the realist's painting, which maintains the illusion that knowledge can be painted exactly as it is "seen" from some external source, and that it must maintain its "pure" state regardless of the learner's subjective interpretation. In this design and practice of education, the false binaries between subject and object reify the modernist notion that "reality" is fixed and somehow independent of our subjective landscapes. This perception removes the "I" (or subjectivity) from the eye of meaning making and offering conjectures that there is one Truth "out there" to be known.

For example, one of the aims of standardized testing is to supposedly ensure that all students convey understanding of material each in exactly the same fashion, much as observers might be expected to view a painting through one single window of meaning. Therefore, the value behind such a technical design is to shape knowledge and students towards a form of understanding and expression that guarantees accountability and homogeneity.

A left-handed, (aka *critical post avant-garde*) curriculum serves as a representation, or a window, into ourselves: an intersection between audience and autobiography, where we might arrive at new visions. In this left-handed framework:

> Students experience curriculum, interact with it, transform it, by merging various and unique contextual realities within a multitude of frameworks of time and space/place . . . (students) cannot be separated from the unique context in which they are being understood. They are always perceived, their meaning re-constructed, from a particular angle or reference point. (Slattery, Krasney, & O'Mally, 2007, p. 538)

Learning, like art, can be interpreted as a fluid process in which the "I" and eye (McDermott, 2011) create a third space that exists in the process in between the two. A methodology, or "style," for understanding curriculum, one that emphasizes the correspondence between the object and the self, becomes a way to reconsider the relationship between learner and curriculum. We might reconsider, like Molyneaux (1997), a design and interpretation of learning that is "situated and dynamic, changing as the material and social landscape changes" (p. 113). Like the relationships between art, artist, and audience, we must ask, "But what of the students' relations to the selected objects of curriculum?" (Sumara & Davis, 1998, p. 4). We might look at style as processes of correspondence towards the creation of an emergent product.

These "collaged" relationships, in correspondence with one another, become ever-emerging spaces of shape shifting, where the aesthetics of meaning and the construct of experience hold the power to transform. In terms of curriculum, such correspondences elicit a move towards a fluid, interactive, and multitextual conception of relationships. Curriculum and person become mutually shaping elements in the development of sociocultural beliefs and practices. By reexamining the design and presentation of material knowledge within an educational context using an aesthetic lens, we can stand back from the familiar, the "taken for granted" assumption that certain values and perceptions are fixed "natural" realities. We might instead consider the following question: Who benefits from this specific codification and arrangement of knowledge or experience?

By aesthetically reconceiving curriculum as an object embedded with style we witness the familiar becoming strange. Pinar (1998) explores this process as a "voyage out" that takes us away from the habitual and the taken-for-granted, instead engaging us in a curricular experience that is open to what is not known and unpredictable. An analysis of style peels back the layers hardened over by our taken-for-granted ways of seeing ourselves and others. Instead we can allow for a curriculum that "feels risky, dangerous, forbidden—for within it, we are able to imitate nothing but who we are" (Sumara & Davis, 1998, p. 2). Such movement feels risky or "dangerous."

Educators need to consider that "we are pervaded by the beliefs of our own social groups—nation, locality, class, religion, politics, occupation, gender, age, race, ethnicity—beliefs in the form of assumptions that we make unconsciously" (Prown, 1982, p. 4). By engaging in a critical analysis of the aesthetics of curriculum design, examining styles of meaning-making, we can uncover layers of assumptions, transforming the unconscious into the conscious. Castillo, author of *Left-handed Teaching* (1974) states, "To teach is to show the child that more is possible" (p. 39). My book builds on that notion, and adds that in order to do this, teachers must be able to work from a left-handed curriculum to see that more is possible as well.

Teach dangerously and implement curriculum with style, and learning becomes an aesthetic experience, a dangerous style forged within the context of lived experience. The learning process, like art, should "draw on and from the materials of their (students) daily world, and working with them idiosyncratically, produce in the process a new relationship between art and the world, a new way of being in the world" (Berger, 1985, p. 159). We transform ourselves into agents of change through the creative application of technique and aesthetic analysis. Education becomes a dangerous thing. But more than an object of "art," curriculum is a visceral map of our cultural and social landscape, a metaphoric and literal representation of particular values and beliefs.

Putting it All Together

Bringing this all together—aesthetics, art, creativity and curriculum—in a different light, one in which the concepts are interchangeable and mutually shaping, I hope that my readers, as they move onward to Part II to engage with art-ful curricular experiences themselves, will keep in mind the power of creativity to empower change. As such, the ideas in this book share some commonalities with what Gaztambide-Fernandez (2010) calls "creative solidarity" in the field of curriculum work. He states that curriculum workers ought to be "at least deeply troubled by the rise in the United States of policies like those found in the No Child Left Behind Act and their mixed bag of implication for the mostly poor communities of color" (p. 85).

In an effort to dismantle this oppressive educational landscape, those working in the field of curriculum (and to his definition I would include teachers like those to whom this book is dedicated) might work in solidarity, as creatively and collectively conceived, a process that "might yield visions of what is possible; a language of the imagination" (Gastambide-Fernandez, 2010, p. 86).

I suggest that the most powerful and far-reaching changes occur within *communities*, whether they are school communities or neighborhoods. A critical post-avant-garde style for curriculum, like art of the same title, embraces (rather than erases): our lived social contexts; social, political, and ecological issues as being the center of the work; collaborative approaches to the design and styles of teaching we may create; and embodied/sensory ways of being with each other and the world.

Empowering teachers to work together to be creative as human beings encourages them to become more empowered as educators when they come together with an educational purpose. Teachers, like artists, working creatively and collaboratively can do what the work of one individual cannot: to change worlds, educational or otherwise. As Goldbard (2006) posits: "What can art do? One artist's dream can't end a war, but when enough people dream together—when enough people have a taste of wide-awake dreaming to create critical mass—who knows what might happen?" (p. 14).

1. Close your eyes and imagine your classroom on any given day. Moving from images to words, or words to images (which ever you prefer), create a list of descriptive words and a quick easy sketch both of which depict the *aesthetic qualities* of your classroom. (Workspace available on next page). Include your students, the curriculum—as broadly defined here, your teaching *style,* and the actual physical space in which you teach. The drawing and description can include both what is felt/experiences as well as the literal physical attributes of the space/course of events. Don't worry about making a realistic picture! Think like an abstract artist and focus simply on basic elements of design, and what the drawing symbolizes. No stick figures needed.

Helpful hints:

Think of descriptive terms such as: loud, crowded, hectic, smooth, organized, seamless, busy, confusing, over burdened, playful, predictable or spontaneous.

Use the basic elements of design:

Lines:

Dots:

Shapes:

(a)   (b)   (c)

Color:

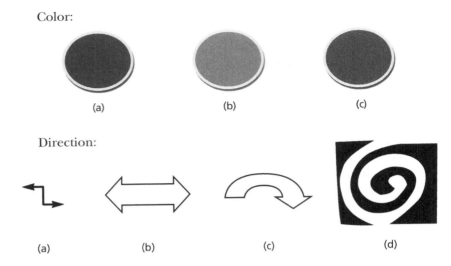

Direction:

(a)   (b)   (c)   (d)

Use the basic design elements in your sketch as these elements to reflect (or inspire) your descriptive words.

2. When you are done, consider the following questions in self-reflection or in discussion with others: Are the words and image as you would like them to be? What would you change if you could? How do the sketch and the word list expand your own conceptions of curriculum, creativity, and art, as each influence your identity as an educator? Looking at the chart on page 29, are your curriculum design and teaching style more Modern or Postmodern? In what ways did the discussion in Part I add to or alter your existing assumptions about teaching and learning?

Note

1. Gestalt is a German word meaning both the whole (as being more than the sum of its parts), and the pattern. http://edinburgh-gestalt-institute.moonfruit .com/#/what-is-gestalt/4509313638

Sketch:	Descriptive Words:

PART **II**

Theory into Action

1

Curriculum As Space

Theory

I've listed the qualities that a school would want to evoke: that it would be fun and respectful; that it would inspire wonder; that it would enable creative play, individually and in groups. A school should engender a sense of community. There should be age-appropriate tools and resources. There should be a physical building that provides nurture and protection.
—(Raffi, in OWP Architects et al. [Eds.], 2010, p. 32)

Curriculum is not only what we teach but how, and *where*, we teach. While schools (public, private, charter, magnet, or otherwise) are considered the formal spaces we inhabit for teaching and learning, the idea of curriculum *as space* connotes the three-dimensionality of our human interactions. Knowledge and meaning-making occur not in vacuums, nor via direct transferences via the "banking model" (Freire, 2000) from paper to a child's mind, or vice versa. We can no longer default to modernist "curriculum models and pedagogical approaches that assume students...can simply inhabit generic spaces without concern for their complex, individual subjectivities" (Carpenter & Springgay, 2011, p. 98). Rather, we co-create experiences for teaching and learning that are contingent upon many factors including the spatial relationships in which they occur. So, to re-envision the craft of teaching, we must also explore what we define as spaces where learning becomes manifest.

A traditional classroom space usually includes four walls, maybe some windows, desks/tables, chairs, and certain learning spaces like a reading nook or rug situated in front of a white/blackboard. Most modern American schools consist of winding interconnected hallways and defined spaces for other activities such as a cafeteria, gymnasium, and media center. Such spaces regulate or shape both the ways in which how those spaces can be used and how people can move through them. According to de Freitas (2011):

> We relate to buildings in complex embodied ways. Our individual and collective identity is formed in relation to the many rooms and corridors and entrances we occupy and traverse.... Buildings play a crucial role in our daily lived experience, and in our sense of belonging to particular communities of practice (de Freitas, 2007). (p. 209)

While traditional and rather generic structural designs persist in most public educational institutions, Diamond and Mullen (1999) explain, "we can each ready ourselves to be awakened to the ongoing creation of different worlds—of self, research, and classroom" (p. 9). Space is a *relational* concept. What you see and how you move are always contingent upon the position from which you are standing, the direction toward which you wish to move, and the spaces allotted to do so. There are borders and boundaries that define the spaces we inhabit. There are pathways, bridges, and roads (both literally and metaphorically speaking). The question is not only what spaces *do*, but how we will choose to move ourselves, our students, and our community *through* these spaces. What are they intended for? As Applebaum (2000) states, "the crucial question is how the space is related to as an object, and what is done with and through the space" (p. 37).

In his exploration of what is called the "hidden curriculum of space," Cardoso (2011) explains that there are key tenets to understanding how space shapes teaching and learning:

> Relatively little attention has been given to analyzing the influence of the spaces provided in schools on educating. Teachers' rooms may indicate a great deal about them and their views of education. Many teachers show limited environmental competence: room arrangements often fail to back up the teachers' intentions. Buildings may outlast the theories of education

on which their design was based, and create problems for later users who have different ideas. (Meighan & Harber, 2007, cited in Cardoso, 2011, n.p.)

The hidden curriculum includes facets (or qualities) of "space" that convey hidden, unspoken, tacit, or even unconscious messages about what is experienced, and how, within that space. What messages are conveyed through uses of space to the members of that community about who has power? *Who* is valued in that space? *What* is of value to learn? And what *methods* of learning are included or excluded by the parameters of the space?

In keeping with this notion of space and a hidden curriculum, we might consider that schools are often negatively associated with prisons, spaces in which students (and often teachers) are seen as the inmates, placed under constant scrutiny and threat of punishment. School-as-prison spaces are designed for maximum control and limited autonomy. As Foucault (1979) illustrates in his reference to the *panopticon*, which could be described as the "all-seeing eye" used to maintain existing power relationships imposed by those in power through means of surveillance, a school community is "confined to spaces that are prescribed and regulated" (Diamond & Mullen, 1999, p. 257). As such, "the prisoner, and icon of oppression is seized, confined, and held captive in the restrictive and/or expansive space of a surveillant community" (p. 259).

Changing the dynamics of power relationships within education and breaking free of the prescribed control from top-down, punitive-based approaches to teaching are integral to the creative reimagining of classroom spaces and thus what students and teachers are "free" to do within these spaces. Therefore, taking creative initiative over the literal and metaphorical structure of the spaces we inhabit is vital to "breaking out" from confining institutionalized models that have historically been associated with schooling: prisons and factories (factory model of schooling). The institutionalized model, according to Foucault, developed at the end of the 19th century is

cited in the [then] new institutions of the modern world, from schools and hospitals to workshops and prisons, infiltrating and shaping what is said and done. Its purpose is to produce human beings as 'docile bodies' through the power of administrative regimes and the expertise of professionals. (Gazetas, 2003, p. 197)

However, classrooms do not *have* to be designed in this image. What a left-handed curriculum empowers teachers to do is to create cracks, inroads, or ruptures in the discourse of power. First, though, teachers must begin by imagining what spaces for teaching and learning *could* look like, and then imagine little (and big) ways to redesign their spaces that reflect their new visions and creating spaces for alternative possibilities. Space is always negotiable—unfixed. Applebaum (2000) reminds us:

> Perhaps then we could declare space an edifice: something that people build or craft, like a cathedral or a bridge. A Chicano Studies Center, a social studies classroom, or a feminist mathematics classroom may become for us a spiritual place, a connecting arch from one world to another, a platform for political posturing. Now we can begin to talk about repairing the space, or desecrating it, or destroying it. Some spaces become closed or under construction. In a Foucauldian moment we become intellectual terrorists, and blast open the conceptual bridges of common sense in order to make it possible for new edifices constructed out of the rubble of the ruins. (p. 40)

The spaces and places represented in a left-handed curriculum are multiple and complex aesthetic compositions, drawn from the invisible (and often ignored) experiences and knowledges, to be seen and given consideration. To do so is to honor the value and relevancy of these spaces and the ways they affect larger issues in social and educational arenas.

THEORY INTO ACTION: *From Boxes to Bubbles*

Time needed: 45 minutes for drawings and discussion, and
                60 minutes for bubble construction and discussion

Materials list:

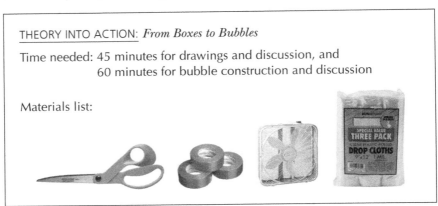

"Drawing" on Creative Spaces

One of the first things I do when I invite teachers to open themselves to the creative process is to ask them what they feel is their ideal space for teaching and learning to occur. Note, I deliberately do not ask them to construct their ideal *classrooms*, because the purpose is to invite teachers to consider how classrooms are but one space for education to manifest, and that thinking outside that space will enable them to free their own minds of longstanding, fixed ideas about what a classroom "is" or can be.

We begin by discussing basic principles of aesthetics: how things feel, sound, taste, or look. I ask them to brainstorm how qualities of light, open/closed physical structures, rhythm, pace, and relationships of self to space and self to others in that space shape what will define the educational experience for both teacher and learner. If you have completed the warm up in Part 1 of this book already, then you have a good beginning to this activity.

Space is an aesthetic, embodied, and sense-based concept. So we begin by highlighting those facets of "space" as they influence our being. For example, jagodzinski (1992 [in Pinar, Reyonolds, Slattery & Taubman, 1995]), notes:

> Texture "is the conversation with 'things' to enable tone to know them intimately." ... In schools texture speaks, "to the need for recognizing the distinctive style that has emerged." Size represents the, "lived experience of scale" ... Mass is, "the lived experience of gravity informed through the binary oppositions between gravity (permanence) and lightness (moveability)." ... Space is defined as, "the lived experience of the cosmos," and in this sense curriculum represents the "architecture of a culture." (p. 490)

Then, using various drawing materials such as markers, crayons, and pastels, and one 8" × 11" piece of white paper, the participant-teachers illustrate their ideal learning space.

Ideal Learning Space, oil pastels and paper, 2010.

This illustration, made by an art teacher from Georgia, reminds me of the words espoused by Copperthwaite (2007), who writes, "[Putting] children behind a desk and make[ing] them stay quiet and inactive for long periods of time from very early years, insisting that they learn the material that is unrelated, for the most part, to their lives in any way they can see" (p. 7). He adds that what children yearn for is "excitement and physical challenge through work and through living close to the natural forces of wind and sea" (p. 7). Of course, the illustration used as an example here does not suggest that this, or any teacher, will simply now go out and open a classroom or school located in a pagoda by a lovely waterfall. This is not an exercise in designing new spaces *literally* in terms of finding quality real estate. Instead, following the drawing exercise, we discussed as a group what qualities this illustration embodied, such as openness, tranquility, peace, experiencing connections to nature, and how learning occurs all around us.

So what could this teacher do to work with the reality of what he's "got" in terms of his more traditional boxed-in classroom with four walls and 24 desks? In this one instance, he and my whole teacher cohort considered how he could bring in a sound machine with a recording of a peaceful waterfall and play it during quiet work time. He could bring the class outside more often (weather permitting) and hold class in the school garden or under a tree. He could bring in one of the smaller sized Zen meditation gardens or fountains where water ripples over small rocks to add a more peaceful element to his class space. He could broaden the curriculum scope of what knowledge is of value, and open the processes of learning beyond the classroom walls.

Most importantly, this teacher cohort examined how the aesthetics of the space could shape his *style* for teaching. Examining more closely the waterfall drawing in terms of its simplest design elements, we can also conclude that this teacher desires a curriculum that has few if any straight lines, or discrete (separate) parts. The lines in his drawing are very fluid, as is the suggestion of the waterfall. The colors in the drawing are blended together as well. In the entire image, without even considering its literal content, one can ascertain the soft, interconnected, and organic qualities of the form, shape, and color, all of which can be transposed onto a style of teaching and learning, making the space of interactions very different than those of a more traditional classroom setting.

In our class discussion I posed questions such as: Where can we create open and peaceful spaces within our curriculum? Where can we make learning more nature-centered or self-reflective? How can such qualities as these shape what and how we teach math or social studies? The answers of course varied, contingent upon the needs and desires of the teacher, the individual students, the classroom community, the subject material, and other socio-geopolitical factors of the community where the students live. Over the years, other drawings have included spaces with more windows, no desks, round walls, or even a garden. In some form or another, many of these ideal qualities are possible within our existing frameworks. We just have to be creative in finding ways to make them happen.

The ambiguity of spatial factors places a lot of responsibility for critical and rich thinking upon the teacher. There is no one-size-fits-all model for reimagining space. First, teachers must become comfortable with notions of emergence and risk-taking as central elements to creative design. Therefore, I take them through the experience of building the bubble.

Building the Bubble

Following the drawing warm-up exercise, I always make building "the bubble" the first experience in the sequence of creative experiences for teachers. On the one hand, it takes off all the pressure to have to know anything, to have right answers, or to be artistic in anyway. The only requirement is some level of participation. And you cannot do this wrong. In an educational world where everything has been boiled down to one right answer, and, in the words of Sir Ken Robinson (2006) "mistakes are the worst thing you can make," (n.p.), allowing teachers to simply "let go" and experiment is vital.

I give much credit for the idea behind this activity to the late Elijah Mirochnick, who was my mentor at Lesley University and one of the most creative and inspiring teachers I have ever known. In the year 2000, I was shadowing him during his Curriculum Theory, Design, and Assessment course, as part of my own training process. During his class he had teachers (new and seasoned) build a bubble out of large plastic sheeting. I will refrain here from explaining how he did this, because it becomes a spoiler for anyone reading this to do the activity themselves.[1]

Having borrowed Elijah's idea once for my own class, I was prepared to use it again in my next Creative Arts and Learning cohort in 2001. But right before I gave the instructions on how to build the bubble to my class I was struck by an idea: What if they had to figure out for themselves how to use these materials to build the bubble? What would happen? So rather than giving them the instructions I informed the group:

> You have two 1-millimeter thick sheets of clear plastic sheeting (10 × 25 ft.), two rolls of duct tape, a few pairs of scissors, and a large box shaped floor

fan. Your task, should you choose to accept it, is this is to build a structure that inflates big enough for all of you (there were about 20 teachers) to climb in and out. The rules are: it must be free standing, no hands or bodies needed to keep it in place, you cannot attach it to walls, ceilings or furniture, and it must be inflated. Go.

Then I stood back, and watched, and held my breath. What if they bombed this completely? What if they refused? The hardest part for me, as the teacher in this situation, was letting go. What if the whole class broke out into chaos and disorder? None of those things happened, and in the ten-plus years I have been doing this (to a total of about 30 plastic bubbles) *not one* group has failed to achieve successful completion of the task. Some may take longer than others. I don't answer any questions regarding the correctness or wrongness of their process or design. I refrain from comment. I watch. I observe how the groups work together. I notice who is taking a lead and who is stepping back. I reflect on where in the steps they may run into trouble or when disagreement among participants occurs.

When the bubble is completed, we all climb, or step, inside the structure and discuss the process using the following guiding questions:

"What happened?" Naturally, the participants feel a great sense of pride in their accomplishment. They start with skepticism (usually) and end with triumph.

"What did this process have to do with curriculum?" Invariably, the same sorts of themes have emerged after ten years (and 30 rounds) of discussion. The elements most often cited include: experimentation, trial and error, teamwork, collaboration, permission to make mistakes, open-mindedness, and innovation.

We also consider other questions such as, *"What was important in this process?"* or *"How does building the bubble relate to teaching and learning?"*

The purposes of this activity are many—each layered and overlapping. In an era of standardization, right and wrong answers, and linear approaches to learning (a, to b, to c . . .) there is little room left to embrace those vital qualities of experimentation, trial and error, teamwork, collaboration, permission to make mistakes, open-mindedness, and innovation. Yet these skills are vital to preparing children for the 21st century as democratic citizens in a complex world.

Furthermore, what makes this process different than simply giving the instructions for building the bubble is that the task becomes entirely participant-centered. Each bubble-builder must work in collaboration with one another. I am no longer the harbinger of knowledge (as the teacher).

Rather I am illustrating to these participants that they are capable of knowledge building and meaning making on their own, drawing on their own knowledges and skill sets in creative ways. In our discussions, the teachers and I consider how little autonomy we give to K–12 students. I usually ask, "*What would happen if you 'let go'? If you trusted your students to arrive at an understanding of whatever you're teaching, even if they get there a different way than you expected?*" Such questions remind me of the work of Nachmanovitch (1990), who reminds us:

> The power of mistakes enables us to reframe creative blocks and turn them around. Sometimes the very sin of omission or commission for which we've been kicking ourselves may be the seed of our best work.... The troublesome parts of our work, the parts that are most baffling and frustrating, are in fact the growing edges. We see these opportunities the instant we drop our preconceptions and our self-importance. (p. 137)

One common emotion that arises in these discussions is fear, because "fear of judgment, fear of failure, and frustration ... are society's defenses against creativity" (Nachmanovitch, 1990, p. 138). Fear pervades classrooms today, as teachers are under even greater pressure than ever before to ensure their students perform well on tests. As such, there is little room for risk-taking on behalf of either student or teacher. And a great deal to be lost individually and as a society as a result.

Can making illustrations of an ideal classroom space, and building a bubble, followed by a critical conversation about the hidden curriculum of space allow educators to re-envision sites for teaching and learning that invite risk-taking, student-centered experiences, collaborative and community-driven efforts, and the courage to make new discoveries? Teachers are less and less likely under the new paradigm of fear and "accountability" to experiment with the existing prepackaged curriculum. My hope is that having this experience will remind educators of the greatest powers they possess within themselves, and to reawaken their own capacities for risk-taking and exploration, to feel again what it's like to trust their intuition, to work creatively with one's peers, to have fun, and to have *faith* (faith in each other, oneself, and the process).

The bubble as a *space*-building exercise reminds us that space can be something we imagine, create, and inhabit together—something that is emergent and fluid. What we do and who we are, are intricately interwoven with the spaces in which we move. Applebaum (2000) argues that "space is something which is always there and always experienced" (p. 41), so the question remains: Will we continue to allow them (spaces) to shape us?

Or, will we begin to create avenues to shape them in accordance with the visions we wish to embody?

This is the first "aha" moment teachers need to have if they are to encourage such experiences in their own classrooms. I don't believe this is something you can simply tell people to do. Everyone must build their own bubble first, to really appreciate within their own sense-making and their unique embodied experience, the value of this *process* rather than the proscribed outcome.

Note

1. An image of a completed bubble has been intentionally excluded so that readers will not be influenced by the design ideas of others when they attempt to perform this exercise themselves.

CURRICULUM AS SPACE WORKPAGE

Questions to Consider and Discuss Following the Completion of These Two Experiences

1. Compare/share your drawings of an ideal learning environment with each other. What similarities do you find? What differences? As a group are you discovering common themes about what you all feel is important in defining an ideal space? Brainstorm possible changes to your classroom and school-wide environment that would support your discoveries.

2. What group dynamics were apparent during the Build a Bubble activity? Did you uncover anything unexpected about yourself or others? What strengths did each person bring to this experience? How could your school community tap into these strengths in more creative ways? What might be accomplished?

3. How does the bubble building experience (both process and product) relate to creative processes that already exist, *or need to be more present,* in your curriculum? List some ways you might embrace these creative processes more in specific lessons or content areas.

2

Building Catapults and Community
Aesthetics of the Transitory

Theory

"Chris" from *Northern Exposure* (1992): I've been here now for some days, groping my way along, trying to realize my vision here. I started concentrating so hard on my vision that I lost sight. I've come to find out that it's not the vision, it's not the vision at all. It's the groping. It's the groping, it's the yearning, it's the moving forward. I was so fixated on that flying cow that when Ed told me Monty Python already painted that picture, I thought I was through. I had to let go of that cow so I could see all the other possibilities. Anyway, I want to thank Maurice for helping me to let go of that cow. Thank you, Maurice for playing Apollo to my Dionysus in art's Cartesian dialectic. And thanks to you, Ed, cause the truth shall set us free! And Maggie, thank you for sharing in the destruction of your house so that today we could have something to fling. I think Kierkegaard said it oh so well, "The self is only that which it's in the process of becoming." Art? Same thing. James Joyce had something to say about it too. "Welcome, oh life! I go to encounter for the millionth time the reality of experience, and to forge in the smythe of my soul the uncreated conscious of my race." We're here today to fling something that bubbled up from the collective unconsciousness of our community. Ed, you about ready? The thing I learned folks, this is absolutely key: It's not the thing you fling. It's the fling itself. Let's fling something, Cicely!

—*Northern Exposure* (1992), Burning down the house [episode]

The Left-Handed Curriculum, pages 51–61
Copyright © 2013 by Information Age Publishing

51

Northern Exposure is a television series that aired during the early 1990s based on the lives of quirky and likable characters living in the fictional town of Cicely, Alaska. In one particular episode called "Burning Down the House" (1992), Chris, the resident "Renaissance man" has the artistic inspiration to create a "pure moment" by flinging a live cow through the air in a giant catapult. His idea is stymied when he discovers, after talking with his friend Ed, that Monty Python had already flung a cow in the movie *Monty Python and the Holy Grail* (1974). Chris states sadly that "repetition is the death of art," and therefore he cannot fling a cow. Later in the show, he realizes that transformation may be a solution to avoiding repetition in the creative process.

Meanwhile in this same episode, Maggie, a young feminist bush pilot is visited by her very yuppie, and "perfectly nice," mother from Grosse Point, Michigan. She announces to Maggie that she and Maggie's father are getting a divorce, and then proceeds to accidentally burn Maggie's house down. The divorce leaves Maggie questioning her memories of a happy childhood, and how this change will dramatically affect previous conceptions of her own identity. Maggie shares with a friend after receiving the news of the divorce that she now realizes that she "spent her whole life rebelling against something that didn't even exist."

What the various subplots woven together in this episode reveal are the ways that emergence, collaboration, and transformation can shape our creative conceptions of self and the world around us. These themes relate to an experience I do with teachers, in which we explore how "aesthetics of the transitory" influence what can and could be revelatory in a left-handed curriculum. The themes and events of this *Northern Exposure* episode directly parallel the themes that ground my notions of critical post-avant-garde arts-based teaching and learning.

Collaboration

The events in the episode weave together an emerging pattern of interrelationships. From the beginning of the storyline, despite his quandary over the "originality of art," Chris recognizes the community itself is embedded in his artistic venture. Local farmers bring cows by for Chris to use for the catapult. Following the demise of this idea, after Maggie's house burns down, Chris has an epiphany. He stumbles across Maggie's "burnt and destroyed Mason and Hamlin [piano] which was never, and now will never be in tune." He decides instead to fling the piano. At the "flinging ceremony" he acknowledges the role that everyone had in creating this artistic moment. He thanks Maggie for sacrificing her destroyed piano to the artistic cause. He thanks Ed for showing him "the truth" by telling him about

Monty Python. Finally he says, "Today we are going to fling something that has bubbled up from the collective unconsciousness of our community." This episode reflects the premise in art-as-community that "to redefine and redesign what communities mean is one thing, but to take an active role in such transformative practices by actually living within the context of the situation is another" (Carpenter & Springgay, 2011, p. 99).

Emergence

Chris, quoting Soren Kierkegaard, proclaims that, "The self is only that which is in the process of becoming.... Art? Same thing." It is in moments of transition that we can step back from the routine, from the taken for granted, and reassess who we are and to allow other possibilities to emerge. Maggie's mother drives that point home when she gets the divorce. She is going through a period of change, venturing into the unknown of who else she might become. In the last scene Maggie asks her mother what she plans to do next. With a wry Cheshire Cat smile, her mother replies, "I really don't know." Both the divorce and the destruction of her house leave Maggie questioning just about everything about her own identity as well.

When Chris stumbles across Maggie's piano in the burned down rubble, he has a revelatory moment. He says, "You look and you look, but you don't know what you're looking for, or if it even exists. And then ... boom." Emergence implies that often we cannot truly "see" what we are actually looking for, and that by stumbling about in the unknown, and through "chance" encounters, sometimes we discover things we couldn't have hitherto even imagined.

Emergence is also about "something else" rising up from the old, an idea in keeping with Gablik's ideas about post avant-garde art in that "nothing new" is being created. Chris realizes that there are no beginnings or ends, just spiraling cycles of transition.

Transformation

Through collective and emergent change comes transformation. This idea is altogether different from the notion of something being "new." From destruction comes creation. "We're standing at the center of the primordial ooze, like the dawn of creation," Chris announces. Maggie replies with cynicism, "This is my living room Chris, not exactly the dawn of creation." He replies, "Don't you understand? It's all about creation and destruction on the scarred battlefield of life." Rather, transformation implies change; that something "was something else" formerly but has now somehow become altered. The burned piano, when flung, became a transitory aesthetic moment. Creation is destruction transformed. When Chris gave up the idea of trying to create something "new" that had never been done before (and failed), he realized that the artist and art actually "transform" one another. Further, the material and the artist transform each other. Following the shift or ruptures in our seemingly seamless existence, we realign the various elements of our being into a different order. Chris states, "From the old skin rises the new snake."

Instead of looking beyond or outside of ourselves, we might take what is already in front of us through our collective visions and belief in "the emergent," and to tap into the transformative power of art (and teaching–learning). From the destruction in our world, from the social ills and ecological concerns, we may create transformative ways of thinking and engaging with the world around us (McDermott, 2005). As teachers, can we "burn down our own houses" in order to create something that perhaps is better suited to our changing times and global need? This requires a breaking of old patterns and frames, of old definitions and beliefs that no longer serve their purpose. It also requires *our own* active, critical, and creative engagement. We cannot allow others to do it for us. As Maggie's mother warned her, "Don't wait for someone else to burn down your house. You do it. Rip it up by the roots. Go out there and meet your life."

The phrase, *the aesthetics of the transitory*, is a ten-dollar way of defining those things in our craft of teaching that move around us and within us every day. It's developing an awareness of our senses and acquiring a different way of seeing our lived and embodied contexts. What if we were to approach teaching and learning the way that Chris approached his process of flinging he piano? What might change? Can we learn to let go of the "cow" (whatever that might be for each of us) so that we might discover the "piano" as something other than what it used to be, using the ideals of collective knowledge, emergent style, and transformative aims as our guides? Like the fling itself, I hope to convey the notion that creative reimagining

---

THEORY INTO ACTION

Time needed: Approximately 3 hours for watching the *Northern Exposure* episode (45 min), construction of catapult, and a flinging ceremony/discussion

Materials: Recyclables and "junk" such as 2 × 4 wood boards, hangers, wire, nails, glue guns, paint, rubber bands, aluminum, egg cartons .... Anything!

of our curriculum, what we are representing and creating is, as Chris puts it, an "aesthetics of the transitory."

The interwoven storylines of *Northern Exposure* embody the central tenets for creativity I feel need to be articulated within the field of education (McDermott, 2004). I want the teachers I work with in my Lesley University graduate classes to have first-hand experience with the process that Chris had in *Northern Exposure*. So during our class time we watch this episode of *Northern Exposure*. Before watching it, I ask, "What do you think the 'aesthetics of the transitory' means?"

Clearly this phrase feels daunting, so I break it down. I ask, "What does aesthetics mean?" Several responses include, "Beauty, art, what we see, how something makes us feel, the senses..." I pose the question: "What does transitory mean?" Possible responses usually include: "Things not permanent, something in motion, change, and movement."

The bigger question I then pose is this: "So what is it in our curriculum (as defined in the first section of this book) that we can consider *aesthetic* and *transitory?*"

Prior to class I ask all teachers/grad students to bring in junk objects, recyclables, and everyday household objects with an eye toward building a "catapult." Objects that can serve as strong bases and springs for flinging should be considered. While it would easy to simply to go to any craft store and buy the materials new, or a model catapult from any toy store, to do so is missing the point. Like Chris, who saw hitherto unimagined possibilities for the now destroyed piano, I want my participants to reimagine other uses for "junk" or everyday objects. The point is to use our imaginative capacities to see things as they might be transformed.

In small teams of four to six people, these teachers create catapults. Like the bubble building experience, there are no directions to do this. The group must use trial and error, experimentation, and teamwork to arrive at their final product. The only two rules are: It must be free-standing (cannot function only when held in your hand like a sling shot), and it must actually FLING something about the weight of a penny or more.

The processes involved in the construction of the catapults become the foundation for discourse about the aesthetic qualities that make for vital democratic curriculum as well. The teachers and I explore how scrap objects parallel (like the piano) the ways that factory models of schooling and high-stakes testing discard students' lived experiences; cultures; issues of race, class, gender; and other differences as being valuable curricular considerations.

Teacher-made catapult, 2005.

Teacher-made catapult, 2007.

After completing the catapult, each group/team reflects on the following questions (samples of previous teacher responses over the years are included in italics):

1. Think of words and concepts associated with curriculum. List those that you believe you used or applied while creating the catapult:

The following words are concepts associated with curriculum that we also applied while creating our "flinger": Planning, Collaboration, Teamwork, Problem Solving, Trial and Error, Flexibility, Creative Thinking, Purpose, Objective, Goal, Measurable Data, Materials, Time.

2. Think about various qualities about the piano from the video. What could the piano metaphorically represent in education?

   The piano could metaphorically represent the curriculum itself— which some see as worthless, some see as valuable, and some see as somewhere in between. Keeping in mind that "flinging" isn't the same as "getting rid of,"—rather is synonymous with transforming—we chose to "fling" the curriculum because it needs to be revamped, not completely discarded.

3. Relating to what the piano represents in question #2, list 5 "things" (metaphorically speaking) that you would like to fling from your catapult? Why these 5? (Remember: flinging is NOT the same thing as "getting rid of ... ")

   The 5 things we chose to catapult were: Reliance on standardized testing, excess worksheets, pen-and-paper assessments, canned programs, mandated blocks of subject time & departmentalization. We believe that standardized testing shouldn't be used as the sole measure of a student's ability (as it currently is). The amount of time spent on worksheets (paper-and-pencil tasks) could be better spent on hands-on, arts-based activities. Pen-and-paper assessments should be replaced with authentic assessments. Mandated blocks of time and departmentalization fragment the student's day and make it difficult or impossible to integrate and make connections between subject areas and their lives.

4. What might your catapult represent in education/curriculum?

   Our catapult represents "us." We will be the catalyst for change and transformation of our curricula.

5. List what you feel are important "aesthetic qualities" of teaching? Of learning? Relate to the video and various storylines:

   Important aesthetic qualities of teaching and learning include: a balance of staccato and legato styles, flexibility, student-directed, clear, fluid, spiraling, energetic.

6. What is "transitory" in education? Why is "transitory" of value? Think about *process* versus product:

   Transitory—what is always changing in education: What we find valuable and what we think is important for students to graduate knowing is always changing. The powers that be and the people in control are forever in flux as well as popular trends including those in technology and its uses/importance, programs, and strategies. The role of the school in educating a child is transitory—i.e., whole child, the 3 Rs (reading, writing, and arithmetic), character and behavior training, etc.

"Transitory" is of value because it allows us as educators and schools to "be the change we wish to see in education." It allows for reflection and critical analysis of current programs and trends and in turn spurs change and improvement. The process of critical analysis and critical thinking is as important as the transformation itself.

After the catapults have been built, we all participate in a "flinging ceremony" where the teachers get to fling pieces of paper that contain responses to each question or other possible prompts aimed at encouraging them to make connections between the building of the catapults and democratic educational processes.

For example, in response to the direction, "Think of words and concepts associated with creativity. List those that you believe you used or applied while creating the catapult," some groups used words such as: "cooperative, flexible, accepting, experimental [and] functional." One group included similar words such as "teamwork" and "changing." Others had a more structured attitude toward the process and considered words such as "technical and efficient" as important elements, yet they also included elements such as "flexible, weird, and evolving" as significant to the creative process as well.

Groups are also asked to reflect on the various qualities of the burned piano, which, according to character Maggie, was transformed from a "burned and scorched Mason and Hamlin which was never in tune" into a work of art. What things in education similarly could be (or need to be) transformed from rubbish into something of value? Groups listed several items that were of importance to them in their daily practices. One group in 2009 wrote: "curriculum that has to change in response to how society has changed." One group suggested the piano might represent: "harmony, Basal readers, change, and transformation." A third group recognized: "the students we have maybe given up on," "individual learning rates," and "the old piano is transformed."

When I pose the question, "What things need to be flung in education, and why?" teachers first chuckle out loud. After releasing our collective pent-up frustrations and getting a good laugh imagining hurling unsympathetic superintendents or low salaries through the air, I ask them to recall, like Gablik's ideas about post-avant-garde art, how the piano itself was not "thrown out" but rather was "transformed" when it was flung.

Every group over the years has placed assessment/testing on their lists. They also referred to top heavy administration and the lack of pay and benefits as concerns. Many teachers expressed their need to transform the structure of their schools to better accommodate classroom needs such as resources and time, which often get lost in the demand for "too many meetings" and top-down district-level administration, and requiring workshops on the "new and improved methods" being changed almost every year.

If education, and left-handed curricular transformations for that matter, are to reflect democratic principles, we must include lived experiences from classrooms that have been previously marginalized from traditional school design. The making of the catapults is a way to document from "the bottom up" those factors that perpetuate oppressive practices, or those that might become part of a democratic transformation when acknowledged and "thrown into" emergent and collective actions.

I ask teachers to consider what the catapult itself might represent. Reminding ourselves that the catapults are (1) made from scrap objects put together collectively, and (2) act as the "change agents" or flingers of the metaphoric piano, some responses from previous classes include: "Teachers trying to work without support"; "The lift of society to create change"; "Teachers transforming public schools."

Finally, when asked what aesthetic qualities of teaching and learning they felt were of importance they used much of the same terminology used to describe the processes used in creating the catapults. One group said, "Don't be afraid of change" because, "change keeps things relative and meaningful to student's lives."

Another group summarized their educational theory in aesthetic terms as, "taking bits and pieces and putting them together and re-evaluating the process and the product." Using descriptive words such as "rhythm," "tone," and "rate," one group explained that "both teachers and learners need a balance between [these] aesthetic qualities in order to successfully reach learner." It is at this juncture that many teachers begin to make connections between avant-garde art, curriculum, and education. Can we practice a curriculum that is aesthetic and emergent? These are pedagogical approaches that model Chris' purpose, in which he explains to Shelly:

> You see Shelly—what I'm dealing with is the aesthetics of the transitory. I'm creating tomorrow's memories—and as memories, my images are as immortal as art—which is concrete.

I wonder, to what extent are we prepared to approach curriculum as a process by which we create memories, which are as immortal as art, using materials which, like art, are concrete? Additionally, a creative curricular practice requires us to engage in emergent and collective endeavors that incorporate marginalized voices as well as "silences" (McDermott, Daspit, & Dodd, 2003). From the "charred battlefield" (to quote Chris) of daily classroom experiences emerge the fragments of dreams, shadows, experiences, values, memories, fears, and hopes of students and teachers alike, brought together, not in perfect harmony but perhaps in their messy complexities to fling, and to embrace our collective visions for transformation.

Questions to consider and discuss during and following the completion of the catapult experience:

1. Think of words and concepts associated with curriculum. List those that you believe you used or applied while creating the catapult.

2. Think about various qualities about the piano from the *Northern Exposure* episode. What could the piano metaphorically represent in education?

3. Metaphorically speaking, what would like to fling from your catapult? (Remember: flinging is NOT the same thing as "getting rid of...")

4. What might your catapult represent in education/curriculum?

5. List what you feel are important "aesthetic qualities" of teaching? Of learning? If more than one catapult was constructed, what common themes appeared across each of the groups?

6. What is "transitory" in education? Why is "transitory" of value? Why are experiences that are *aesthetic and transitory* of value in learning? Think about *process* versus product.

3

Composition: Exposing the Ordinary

Art is a system of encounters, inter-subjectivities. . . . It advocates an inter-corporeal relationality, a way of knowing [that is] . . . redolent with sensuous knowledge, full of ecstasy and excess. It speaks the language of images and words, smells and textures, sights and sounds. . . . It cultivates breath.

—Springay, 2004, p. 15

Theory

Composition is a term much like curriculum or art, in that it is broad in scope, and may have multiple meanings across various contexts. The definition of the term *composition* for this chapter and the teacher experience it discusses is twofold: (1) as the expression of something to communicate using a particular language system, and (2) as a theatrical technique developed by Anne Bogart.

Composition can be performed using the written word, visual communication, music, and/or movement (choreography), to name just a few. For example, to compose a poem one must use letters, which become words, arranged in a particular way to create meaning. To compose is to make something—that is, something made up of particular "compositional" ele-

The Left Handed Curriculum, pages 63–74
Copyright © 2013 by Information Age Publishing

ments. The arrangement of letters, as well as the structural design of the words or sentences on a page, affects the meaning. Similarly, the composition of a painting is made up of basic elements of visual design including color, shape, direction, and line. The colors as they are arranged across the canvas affect the final product. For example, if you replaced the colors blue and green with neon pink and black, how would the possible meanings of the artwork change? Likewise, in music, basic musical notation is arranged in certain ways, creating a particular expression. Change some facet of the notes, rhythm, or tone and the composition itself is changed. In choreography, a dancer uses levels of space, architecture of the body, and speed of movement (among other elements) to compose a story embodied within the performer(s).

So composition is more than merely writing an essay on what you did last summer. Composition encompasses the basic building blocks of all our aesthetic forms of communication. Through the different artistic choices used by the composer(s), a range of tones, moods, and feelings can be conveyed by the performers and interpreted by the audience/readers. When working with teachers, using composition to explore curriculum from a "left-handed" perspective, I first discuss what the word composition *means*. We refer back to the work completed and discussed while building the bubble and making the catapults as the aesthetic qualities of those experiences relate to the composition of curriculum.

Concepts related to "space" explored in Chapter 1 are also quite relevant. Architecture and other ways of understanding spatial design all use composition as well; one considers how narrow or wide hallways may be, use of natural light through windows, how open or cluttered or confining a space may feel. All depend on elements of composition that affect what people hear, see, or feel in their bodies within a certain space.

As part of our discussion around composition and curriculum, I pose a series of discussion questions such as:

How do the aesthetics of the elements of style affect what can be communicated and how?

How can we begin to make conscious choices over our uses of basic compositional elements to communicate an idea?

In what ways is our understanding of a particular concept informed or transformed by the different types of composition being employed (i.e., how does feeling, communicated in musical notes, relate to color choices in a painting)?

The point of composition work in curriculum is to move in two directions: First the participants move "backwards"—deconstructing what current concepts of curriculum are, by examining basic compositional elements. Second, participants then move "forward," using elements of composition to (re)construct a more creative vision for future curricular engagements.

In class then I introduce Anne Bogart's (Dixon & Smith, 1995) use of composition in her theatrical exercise called *Viewpoints* developed in the late 1970s and early 1980s. Bogart uses Mary Overlie's *Six Viewpoints*: space, story, time, emotion, movement, and shape, to encourage actors to examine how their bodies in space enhance their character development. These six viewpoints, broken down into their basic compositional elements, look like this:

Space

- Architecture—The physical environment, the space, and whatever belongs to it or constitutes it, including permanent and nonpermanent features.
- Spatial Relationship—Distance between objects on stage; one body in relation to another, to a group, or to the architecture.
- Topography—The movement over landscape, floor pattern, design and colors.

Shape

- Shape—The contour or outline of bodies in space; the shape of the body by itself, in relation to other bodies, or in relation to architecture; think of lines, curves, angles, arches all stationary or in motion.
- Gesture—(a) Behavioral gesture: Realistic gesture belonging to the physical world as we observe it every day, and (b) Expressive gesture: Abstract or symbolic gesture expressing an inner state or emotion; it is not intended as a public or "realistic" gesture.

Time

- Tempo—How fast or slow something happens on stage.
- Duration—How long an event occurs over time; how long a person or a group maintains a particular movement, tempo, gesture, etc., before it changes.
- Kinesthetic Response—A spontaneous reaction to a motion that occurs outside of oneself. An instinctive response to an external stimulus.

- Repetition—(a) Internal: repeating a movement done with one's own body, and (b) External: repeating a movement occurring outside one's body.

Emotion

- Psychological or narrative content ascribed to movement.

Movement

- Movement of your body, different ways of moving—for example, jerky versus smooth/flowing versus very slowly or fast; the movement of different parts of your body.

Story

- All of the different elements influence each other and work together, and can "cause" a change in a different element. For example, the shape of your body may carry a certain emotion with it as well—something in the space of your environment may make a story out of what you are doing, etc.
- The actors must focus first on the isolation of each separate viewpoint element on its own, before integrating and working them all together. It's often the case that a performer finds one of the elements comes naturally, and perhaps uses that one element they really understand to access the other elements, which they must work to become more familiar with.

According to Overlie (n.d.):

> I was given the concept that you can use your mind to move and change definitions but it is necessary to ground these thoughts in physical reality. I was taught to use the concepts of systems and logic, not as a set of rules, but to create a fluid dialogue. I learned to respect, rather than to fear deconstruction. This lesson is now articulated again and again in the Six Viewpoints process as a primary tool for creativity. I came to believe that to be a participant in the future you need to discover the discipline of separating the mechanics of the universe. Through these lessons I began to understand that copying was not necessary, not desirable and actually not possible. (n.p.)

If we consider, as I outlined in Section 1 of this book, that curriculum is a socially, historically, politically, culturally, personally, geographically, and collectively complex assemblage of narratives involving what knowledge "is," how meaning is made, and, "what knowledge is most worth" (Spencer, 1861, p. 63), then it follows that curricular narratives are embodied in, and projected from, the aesthetic landscape *performed* in classrooms and communities. While we utilize all of the viewpoints listed above in our daily actions, most of us do so unconsciously. One vital role of the imagination and creativity in education is to provoke what Greene (1995) calls a "wide awakeness" of our beings; composition as an exercise elevates facets of our taken-for-granted actions and assumptions to the conscious foreground, making us keenly aware of how we can, or ought to, shape our classroom practice. In her strategy called "Doing the Unnecessary" Overlie (n.d.) observes that:

> The Unnecessary is based on breaking the habitual use of our senses to fulfill ordinary tasks such as: walking, speaking, reaching, exiting, entering, taking our coat off, or sitting down. When these actions exist in the necessary we produce them through minimal and efficient co-ordinations of our movements, spatial judgment, timing, and appropriate shapes in our bodies. This well-planned achievement leaves out much of our attention to what we are actually doing. This causes our senses to be only half-alive/half-asleep in these actions. The coat, the chair and the body are not fully present. (n.p.)

As a form of curricular exploration, composition work becomes what I call "performative mapping," described in this way:

> We map our experiences, moving landscapes traced with aesthetic and sensory hues, ruptures of memory and overlays of the imagination. Such experiences in turn determine the forms such representative maps will take.... The body of work [curriculum] and the constructor of that work intertwine each other in mutually shaping processes where properties from each are infused into each other. The "original" form and content of the representation cannot remain static, but flows outward and implodes inward unto itself at each intersection in which it is performed. Curriculum, possible interpretations and representational form themselves are transformed by multiple emergent contexts into unpredicted and un-thought of possibilities. (McDermott & Daspit, 1999, n.p.)

Working from Overlie's *Six Viewpoints,* Anne Bogart developed an activity for composing one's theatrical character, in which a scene from a dramatic script must be performed using the following nine criteria:

1. spatial relationships
2. shape
3. kinesthetic response
4. repetition
5. architecture (use of space)

6. tempo
7. duration
8. gesture
9. topography

These nine items become a theatrical way to perform (or embody) the various elements within each of Overlie's six compositional frames.

THEORY INTO ACTION

Time needed: 60–90 minutes

Materials: Access to various indoor or outdoor spaces
              Viewpoints/composition checklist
              Selected readings

So what does curriculum look, sound, move, and feel like as a *composition?* When working with educators, I begin by drawing passages from assigned class readings such those from a book entitled *Reflections from the Heart of Educational Inquiry* (Willis & Schubert, 2000). I have not always assigned this specific book as a graduate class reading, and I have used many other texts over the years. I have found that any curriculum-related reading passage will work for doing this experience. Lyrics and poems work as well. I also have found it beneficial to allow teacher-participants, in small groups of five or six, to identify from the array of readings some particular passage or quote that speaks to *them*, rather than assigning specific quotes. The goal is to find quotes that discuss curriculum, either in the traditional sense or how it ought to be redefined.

Drawing from the selected passages, participants then explore how curriculum is "performed," using the elements of composition. In this way, teachers deconstruct the "unnecessary" actions and assumptions about how learning is enacted, and reconstruct, through aesthetic viewpoints, how curriculum *might* be enacted more creatively. The goal is to transform the words of the text or passage, and the interpretation of the group, into embodied ways of making meaning which are then performed for (or with) others.

Here are some sample quotes from various authors who have chapters in *Reflections from the Heart of Educational Inquiry* (2000) that I have used previously in my classes:

Now this process of selection, this determination that something matters, is the very heart of curriculum. The choosing and naming of what matters and the presentation of those values for the perception and engaged participation of others are the deliberations that constitute curriculum development. (Grumet, 2000, p. 74)

Breaking down the barriers between curriculum and life, in a very general way, describes phases of my own work. When I first entered the field as a graduate student in summer 1969, I was astonished by the obsession with the 'technical' in curriculum development. The absence of life lived in its psychological, political, and cultural dimensions made curriculum a blank canvas. (Pinar, 2000, p. 245)

I do not approach the issue of curriculum design as a technical problem to be solved by the application of rationalized models. Rather, following a long line of educators from Dewey to Huebner, I conceive curriculum as a complicated and continual process of environmental design. Thus, do not think of curriculum as a 'thing', as a syllabus or a course of study. Instead think of it as a symbolic, material, and human environment that is ongoingly reconstructed. (Apple, 2000, p. 213)

To see teachers as more or less caught in a web of structural constraints beyond their control or as individuated professionals operating from a knowledge base that ensures a disengaged competence in students, is to deny our role as moral agents engaged in the re-creation of ourselves and our worlds. (Beyer, 2000, p. 203)

Enacted curriculum often lacks imagination, playfulness, and improvisational features. It allows few divergent narratives to unfold and evolve naturally over time, and rarely is time given to student's imagination, thoughtful reflection, or group development and active negotiation of ideas. In the dramatic unfolding of our inventions and stories, valuable truths about ourselves, our subjects, and our situated-ness can be unearthed and shared. Lines blur between fact and fiction, reality and fantasy, and more nearly reflecting our human condition in dramatic social context. (May, 2000, p. 141)

It helps to find passages that have rich and complex interpretative possibilities, as well as key words or ideas that suggest allusions to *space and movement*, thus giving teachers in this activity something to work with.

Then I pass around copies of a list of items/actions that must be included in each group performance. Each of Bogart's *Nine Viewpoints* is woven into the following criteria:

    a. defined setting—where
    b. clear role for the audience (Voyeurs? Judges? Participants?)
    c. surprise entrance
    d. music from unexpected source
    e. use of extreme contrast
    f. use of 3 of the objects somehow

    g. use of two levels of space

    h. 15 seconds of simultaneous unison action

    i. one key line/sentence from assigned concept

In using (a) though (i) as their guidelines, performers (in groups of 5–7) conceive of ways to "show" their understandings of the selected passage using their bodies in space—aesthetic language systems of composition folded into the viewpoints, to express their interpretations. Looking at the quotes listed above, the reader might have already keyed in to certain words as they could connect with certain viewpoints, such as shape, tempo, rhythm, space, repetition. For example:

> breaking down barriers/choosing/naming/process/
> caught in a web/unearthed/

    Additionally, when creating and performing their composition, teachers sometimes represent the opposite of what is in their written passage. For example, if Wanda May suggests that we need to engage more "playfully" in curriculum, a composition might include members of the group droning the same lesson like, "two plus two is four" as their simultaneous unison action; the facet of the composition that may strongly represent the factory-like approach sometimes used in teaching. Teachers begin to think very abstractly about how each action can be metaphorically represented, using basic compositions of sound, shape, space, and movement. Some possible prompts I use for those needing further illustration include:

> When and where in schools do we reinforce *simultaneous unison action?*

> What *shapes* are most prevalent in classroom design? (i.e., square desks, square walls, square chalkboard, square books, square worksheets, or, lines on a page, lines on a test, desks set up in rows/lines, "line up at the door" and "walk in a straight line"). Thus, if we are to break down these assumed patterns we can begin transforming the shapes we embody in our daily practices.

> What are the primary *levels of space* seen in classrooms and how are they used? (i.e., students are usually all seated, at the same level more or less, with the teacher standing up at higher level).

    Participants are broken up into groups of five or six (larger groups up to seven work best) and given time to plan their composition. Some props are allowed, and I encourage them to explore all available spaces as their disposal in creating their composition. Sometimes stairwells make excellent sites for a playful use of levels of space, while performing a composition outdoors in front of a window with the audience standing inside serves as great way to play on the "windows of public perception" about schools. I have had groups use elevators, an exciting place to include the "surprise entrance." Some groups have performed in hallways, emphasizing the idea that schools often enforce conformity through narrow limited spaces, with one's "back up against the wall."

The most challenging aspect of this exercise for participants is requiring that they "show" ideas rather than relying on literal or verbal explanations or descriptions. *Composition is not acting out a skit.* In fact, *no verbal dialogue is allowed during the performance.* Rather, participants must exhibit, abstractly and metaphorically, certain ideas. Of all the exercises in this book, this one may prove to be the most challenging because it demands that participants really extends their imagination and abstract thinking beyond what is normally expected in daily life.

That's the point.

Teachers doing "15 seconds of simultaneous unison action," 2012.

Because I am constrained by paper and ink, and still photos, within the boundaries of this text, I cannot show my readers a video sample performance of this exercise. So instead I will construct a "screen play" of one example, placing the various compositional elements used in parenthesis so my reader can see how each one was incorporated into the performance itself.

Sample Composition

Text
Working from the quote by Wanda May cited on page 141:

> Enacted curriculum often lacks imagination, playfulness, and improvisational features. It allows few divergent narratives to unfold and evolve naturally over time, and rarely is time given to student's imagination, thoughtful reflection, or group development and active negotiation of ideas. (2000, p. 141)

The Setting—A school building, in one hallway with closed doors on each side and a stairwell at one end and an elevator on the other (defined setting). There are seven members of the Composition team and thirteen "audience" members. There is no speaking during this performance. All communications rely on hand gestures and other body signals.

Actions—The audience is informed through hand gestures by one member of the team to line up against the walls, six or seven on either side, standing immediately next to one another forming two straight lines (defined setting and role for the audience—note the two lines represent a distinct shape as well). Then, from out of one of the classrooms marches the Composition team, all moving in lock-step formation and led by one person at the front, holding a classroom textbook (object 1) above their head, followed by another carrying a chair (object 2). In unison they all march and sing the song sung by the guards in the castle of the Wicked Witch of the West in the *Wizard of Oz*—"Oh we o, ee-oh-wo.." (15 seconds of simultaneous unison action—tempo/duration). They march until their line is parallel to, and in the middle of, the two lines standing against the walls. The leader holds her hand up to "halt," and the second person places the chair down and the leader stands on top of it. She then gestures for the team to sit down "crisscross apple sauce" (two different levels of space/topography). The leader, while standing on the chair, holds the textbook above her head like some holy scripture (gesture), and then opens the book. She begins "reading"—making the Charlie Brown "teacher voice"—"wa wa wa wa." Moments later, singing can be heard from inside the elevator (music from an unexpected source). The elevator doors open and one person leaps out shouting "tada!" (surprise entrance and use of extreme contrast), shouts, "imagination, playfulness, and improvisation!" and then proceeds to skip down the hall waving his arms wildly and singing. When he gets to the groups standing against the walls, he begins pulling audience members off the wall and encourages them to begin dancing and singing too. Then he reaches down with his hands and pulls the team members who are sitting down, to stand up. The leader, still standing on the chair, tosses the textbook to the ground with great deliberation (gesture), pulls paper confetti from her pocket (object 3) and jumps down to join in the dance, tossing the confetti into the air.

It is difficult for those creating the composition to see at the outset the myriad of ways that the Nine Viewpoints and the criteria (a) though (i) in my list actually intersect and overlap. One asset of this activity is that is breaks participants free of linear thinking. Oftentimes they'll begin approaching this process using a checklist, in which each item or criterion is added as a separate item rather than seeing how one simple gesture such as marching and chanting in a straight line accomplishes use of shape, space, sound, duration, and tempo all at once.

Following each group performance, the audience discusses what they thought the composition was about, asking where they saw the application of each criteria (a) through (i), and how each of the Viewpoints was used in a deliberate way to convey an idea.

Of particular interest to me is the role of the "audience." Drawing from Augusto Boal's *Theater of the Oppressed* (2002), I consider with the other participants how the role of the audience often parallels Boal's idea of the "spectactor" (2002)—members of the community/audience who became active agents of a performance rather than merely being bystanders. This idea reminds me that being merely bystanders in education leads us to being complicit in perpetuating decisions and actions forced upon teachers and students "from above." Instead, each of us might consider how and when we make a choice to simply follow directions versus when we might instead to resist—refusing to simply line up, or how to break patterns of oppression and silence witnessed everyday in schools.

In another example of composition work from previous classes, the audience stood inside at a window and watched a performance going on outside. The clear role for the audience represented students "looking in" from the sidelines into a system of education that fails to center itself upon the lives and interests of students themselves, or parents/community members who hold particular perceptions of schooling culture, looking outside in. In this example and others like it, we discuss creative ways to reinvolve the outside world within the closed walls of schools. In the role of the audience, participants share with the performers (who choreographed that particular composition) how effective their choices were in their use of space to effect the role(s) of the audience; articulating their understanding of how education, teachers, and/or curriculum are "seen" when located within a certain situatedness that either limits or broadens one's perspectives. Where we *stand* affects everything about how we negotiate our lived circumstances. We need to reexamine what we deem necessary and *unnecessary* to transform our classrooms.

COMPOSITION WORKPAGE

*Questions to consider and discuss during and following
the completion of the Composition experience. After each
performance, I encourage these as talking points:*

1. Looking over the list of Nine Viewpoints and criteria (a) through
   (i), where did you see (as an audience member) the various elements of composition in this performance? Were each of them
   included? What effect did the uses of these elements have on you
   as a viewer?

2. How could you summarize what this composition was "about"?
   What message was it trying to convey? What was effective (or not)
   in the uses of aesthetic elements to convey its message?

3. If the composition told the story of "what is" within education
   that we wish to change, discuss with the group what you could
   change about the composition to thus change our educational
   habits? In other words, if the composition story used straight lines
   marching to reveal a factory model of education, what could you/
   we do besides march in straight lines? And how/where could you
   alter such linearity in your actual classroom practice?

4. If the composition performance included ideas about how education "ought to be changed" using viewpoint elements to convey
   these ideas, discuss how, when, and where these same aesthetic
   concepts (criteria a–i) could transform your classroom and curricula. Be as specific as possible in identifying actions—leave this
   experience feeling as though there's something feasible you can
   do differently immediately!

4

Self, Curriculum, and Collage

Education must be understood as the process by which we produce knowledge from the materials which we are given. The curriculum must return to its center, within the de-centered identity. Education must reveal the process of production in the exercise of consumption. Now I would argue that one important development of modern art provides is with a model of this process in, say, the collages of the surrealists and dadaists, the affichistes...drawing from and on the materials of their daily world...produced in the process a new relationship between art and the world, a new way of being in the world.

—Block, 1998, p. 135

Theory

Collage is an art form made popular in the early 20th century, notably by the works of Western artists such as Pablo Picasso and Marcel Duchamp (Davis & Butler-Kisber, 1999). Collage typically appropriates (or removes) magazine images, scraps culled from daily life, and any other conceivable form of mass media or trash from their previous contexts and through gradual additions, reassembles them into various recombinations, thus producing visual effects that confound linear or unitary readings of the completed product.

The Left Handed Curriculum, pages 75–90

One of the intentions of collage is to "produce effects of spontaneity, simultaneity, ephemerality, fantasy, and disorientation" (Davis & Butler-Kisber, 1999, p. 4). Collage allows the viewer to see everything simultaneously and to create visual exchanges among the various pieces. In terms of a left-handed curriculum, collage has the effect of rupturing, reflecting, and refracting relationships between aesthetic modes of knowing, language, and meaning-making in curricular practices.

Collage serves as a metaphorical, as well as a literal, practice for redefining curriculum. In keeping with the theory of critical post-avant-garde teaching, collage represents the idea that all knowledges and forms of representation are reassemblages of other thoughts, ideas, and experiences. All of the "fragments" that constitute collectively assembled thoughts and creations build on the idea of relationships. Aesthetic "dialogues" between inner life and outer self, between self and other, between knower and known, and between past and future, are constantly shifting and informing each other into a dynamic collage of thoughts that constitute our "reality." Barone (2000) states that the "tentative relationships between qualities are apprehended," and that "these patterns of qualities present themselves as structured fragments" (p. 195).

As McNiff (1992) suggests, "creation is a collaboration process and an intimate relationship between artists and their materials in which the participants continuously transform one another" (p. 64). Conceiving teaching as a creative act, the self becomes both the process and product of the educational experience. This idea shatters "the mechanistic idea that we can know the world only from the outside, by distancing ourselves from it" (Gablik, 1991, p. 55). The spaces, lines, and fissures that redefine traditionally held boundaries in curriculum ultimately "open up the space of freedom . . . of possible transformation" (Greene, 1995, p. 102). The implications for reimagining curriculum are no greater or smaller than the realization that within this new terrain, the role(s) of teacher and student might also be transformed.

Pedagogy and "self" are inherently intertwined. As previous studies (Barone, 2000; Beattie, 2001; Clandinin & Connelly, 2000) and this book indicate, narrative reflection (artistic or otherwise) provides teachers with the opportunity to critically examine their personal experiences and beliefs as they bear upon their teaching practice. Barone (2000) indicates that to understand this process we need to consider our past in meaningful ways, called "life assertions," in order to inform our future actions. He adds: "We must interpret [this process] in a manner which assumes the presence of an agent, a unified being who is performing the action in the light of a previous history of activities and because of a personal involvement with the world" (p. 123).

Teachers in my classes who participate in a collage-making as autobiography process consistently (over the ten years I have done this experience) have indicated that becoming a "good" teacher requires a process of simultaneously exhuming memories and envisioning futures. They state that being a "good" teacher engages the mind, body, and spirit fully in the practice of ongoing changes and exchanges with others (i.e., students) in the life world of the classroom.

The collages, as artistically constructed narratives, allow teachers to create aesthetic renderings of how they see themselves and their teaching. Greene (1995) contends that engagement with the imagination and art is fundamental to knowing oneself. She says that "to learn and to teach, one must have an awareness of leaving something behind while reaching toward something new, and this kind of awareness must be linked to the imagination" (p. 20). As the collages and narrative reflections about the collage-making process constructed by teachers show, curriculum and education are also about artistic processes that embrace a sense of playfulness, perpetual emergence, and visions of transformation—an art of "becoming" rather than of "being." In exploring self as creative collage process, teachers are defining, or (re)defining, their dangerous "style," which Bukowski (1975) defines as "a way of doing . . . a way of being done" (n.p.).

Collage is one example of a dangerous style that encourages transformation through relational and emergent forms of meaning making. Such transformations, as Freire (1998) reminds us, are the keys to creating democratic and socially just schools. The goal, he reminds us, "is not to transfer knowledge but to create possibilities for the production or construction of knowledge" (p. 30). The extent to which teachers can creatively and critically examine conceptions of "self" as racially, socially, and culturally constructed texts in turn has a ripple effect on the pedagogies that they will incorporate into their classrooms.

According to Mullen (1999), "identity is like a cultural collage, variously arranged and glued together" (p. 150). Furthermore, "by working with refracted self-images and with the support of others, we can critique and transform our teaching and inquiry" (p. 86), leading us to reflect on "what teaching now means to us, what it has meant, and may come to mean," so that we might ultimately "become better able to control its varied outcomes" (p. 86).

Collage images also shatter notions of linearity by inviting viewers to begin "reading" the image at any point. There are all points and none at all, existing simultaneously. In examining this relationship and its creative possibilities Paley (1995) writes that:

> Bricolage (as a technique used in collage) challenges analytic processes that construct descriptions of reality in exclusively discursive ways, making available particular kind of strategy for exploring the expressive possibilities of graphic reference as a primary variable in analytic representation.... Images can be read as text. Text can figure as image. (p. 7)

This process represents the actualization of Alan Block's metaphor of *curriculum as affichiste* (1998). He argues that like the collages of the Dadaists and Affichiste of the 1920s, objects and their meanings are perceptually "removed from their fixed traditional educational settings or identities, and re-assembled" (p. 336) into new and strange juxtapositions. Creative educators, much like avant-garde collage artists, draw on "the materials of their daily world, and working with them idiosyncratically, produce in the process a new relationship between art and the world, a new way of being in the world" (p. 336). Davis and Butler-Kisber (1999) explain that:

> The actual manipulation and construction of space that is done in the layering, weaving, and the juxtapositions of scale and perspective within the collage, serves to push the boundaries of possibility and alter viewpoint of the researcher to confront, for example, hidden issues of bias, or to use these visual metaphors to underscore and elaborate relationships among the data. (p. 16)

Block's collage metaphor reminds us that the aim of creative curricular explorations is to "get lost" from, or, to wander off the path of what is known into the realm of the "odd or unaccustomed perspectives" (1998, p. 339).

Perhaps the best example I have seen of how collaged identity serves as critical analysis for blending and disrupting social, racial, and cultural identities comes from Jessica,[1] one of the original case studies in my dissertation (McDermott, 2001). This study explored how the collage process might encourage beginning teachers to creatively redefine their teacher identities and future classroom practices.

At first glance, when Jessica presented her collage, I assumed it was too "traditional"—secretly disappointed that she had not broadened what I thought were her creative efforts to go beyond poster board and simple images. I was *profoundly mistaken*. As Jessica explained her process and thinking, she revealed a tremendous wealth of critical reflection about who she was as a beginning teacher (an undergraduate preservice teacher at the time this was made), and how who she is will creatively shape the kind of

Jessica, "Making Art from Nothing," 2001 (Paper collage)

teacher she becomes. In our interviews, she shared her feelings of invisibility as a Latina amidst a Midwestern White culture. She said:

> I guess because again, as I was growing up, I didn't see myself represented and that's discussed a lot in our classes at Midwest[2] too. . . . I never saw myself represented in textbooks or stories and things like that. (Jessica, personal communication, September, 2000)

The most powerful revelation in Jessica's collage and her discussion about it were the connections between her personal experiences with school (her own and that of her siblings) and the ways that a dominant culture of schooling conflicts with her own beliefs about diversity, and about the lack of resources for arts in many urban schools. Her philosophy stems from a passion to teach to the "underdogs": Underrepresented and underserviced minority students in the schools. Her collage, its aesthetic composition, and her technique, sharply highlight her goals. In one interview she said:

> Where I live like in southwest Detroit there's a pretty decent amount of Hispanic students and it is actually pretty diverse. My high school was pretty diverse. I would just hope they would find themselves somehow, find themselves represented in the curriculum and then express themselves in any creative way they know how, and then find something they like about attending school so they wouldn't end up hopefully, like my brother and my sister.

The collage process was deliberate, drawing from the work of artist Jorge Rosano. Jessica explained:

> He [Jorge Rosano] basically called it "Paper Art." It was so cool, I mean, there were like... I don't know, like the size of this table, but imagine this on the wall and this picture of construction paper and it was pretty much like the Mexican culture although I think he dealt more with the Aztec culture. So there were like serpents and it always had a story and I don't know what they all meant but... just looking at this art made out of construction paper. Who would have thought that art could be made out of construction paper? He demonstrates for children so they have this big gathering and he demonstrates and pretty much he told us that he really uses a pair of scissors, just like a regular pair of scissors, and it's amazing because he does like the smallest little details and I just can't imagine doing it with just a pair of scissors. It was just done so neat. You didn't see a speck of glue and the paper didn't bubble like when you put layer upon layer. There was none of that. I don't know what his trick was and I didn't get that trick.

According to *Folk Tree*, the history of paper art is rooted in particular cultural origins:

> Only a handful of Otomi Indians in the mountains of Puebla continue this particular type of paper cutting, using it for agricultural and magical purposes. Rosano points out that what he is doing is not papel picado, which arrived in Mexico in the 17th Century via China, but rather is derived from an indigenous Mexican art form.... His work cannot be easily categorized— he takes the simplest of materials and transforms them into elaborate and descriptive pieces of art, unique in every way. (www.folktree.com, n.p.)

During our final interview, Jessica concluded:

> I want to go back and take a picture (of his work) because I don't see it anywhere else. I haven't seen anything like that... just to show students what they can do with paper or something like that. I think some of my students will relate to that kind of thing. (October, 2000)

The Three R's of Collage

The three "R"s: Representation, Recombination, and Rev(ea)lation emerged from my own collage-based research work with Toby Daspit (McDermot & Daspit, 1999) and became the operating framework for my dissertation work (McDermot, 2001). In over a decade since then, in my work with teachers and collage art three R's have become the central guiding themes of this work. I have come to realize that both the collage process and product allow us, as the creators, to embody art as an experience in an unfixed state. As a way to communicate, express, and read both ourselves and the world, the three R's became the fluid framework for how we might convey curriculum as non-linear with artistic qualities. The three R's act as "moving" concepts that create bridges and ruptures between the various pieces of collage work. Each guides the movement between the "things" within a collage.

The question I pose to educators engaged in this collage process is: "How do these things influence each other within a creative collaged context, and to what possible ends?" Representation, recombination and reve(a)lation "create new and unpredictable cycles of thoughts and associations" (Bonami, 1996, p. 12). One R does not lead to another in linear fashion. Rather they (inter)connect in multiple places all at once, making logical comprehension of cause and effect indiscernible.

Re-presentation

McNiff (1992), quoting Nietzsche, notes that "He (sic) is no longer an artist, he has become a work of art" (p. 48). I am reminded of the quote from Chris in *Northern Exposure* discussed in Chapter 2: "Self is that which is in the process of becoming. . . . Art? Same thing."

The body of work (representation) and the constructor of that work intertwine with one another in mutually shaping processes where properties from each were infused into the other. The "original" form and content of the representation do not remain static, but flow outward, and imploded inward, at each intersection in which collage is being recreated. Representation through and in collage does not attempt to "fix" identity but instead represents the (1) relationships and (2) shifting patterns that continuously remake the artist's identity. Ideas and words removed from their original context and assembled in new juxtapositions construct new meanings that often overlap the older ones already set forth prior to the inquiry process. As the ideas are being reframed; unpredicted and spontaneous dialogues between the familiar and the unknown emerge. Wandering off of the mainstream path of what is familiar "can indeed make a person a stranger and able to 'see' as never before" (Greene, 1995, p. 92). This process becomes an integral aspect of the larger left-handed curricular experience and final product.

Reve(a)lation

The "(a)" in revelation implies that things can be revealed, or that lead to revelations. Such reve(a)lations occur in collage mostly through either serendipity or through conversations/sharing with others. Collages, as narrative, "can enable others to enter them imaginatively and to be transformed by them" (Beattie, 2001, p. 170). A significant piece of the process for the collage experience comes in the sharing time after the collages have been created. The first phase, the creative process, is about the relationships between the creator and the materials. The second phase includes the collage itself, no longer as process but as product. The third phase is the time in which all members of the working group share their collage stories with one another.

I cannot articulate enough how powerful this experience is for the participants. Bringing forward those fragmented pieces of our own stories, recombined and narrated, serve as a way to build community, solidarity, empathy, and support for one another. The sharing out is as important a process as the creative art process itself. Sometimes individuals arrange their collage around the idea of a presentation or performance so that the collage "product" itself is not complete until it has been shared with others in a group experience (such as in singing a song).

Recombination

Miller (1996) writes, "The mix, in this picture, allows the invocation of different languages, texts, and sounds to converge, meld, and create a new medium that transcends its original components" (n.p.). One must look at how the pieces *together* form a whole. However, I would add that the "whole" is ever-changing and shape-shifts into multiple combinations. Each element of a collage (in process and product) is mutually shaping and simultaneously occurring, and linearity is replaced with a synchronicity of time and space, experience and memory. Collage as a form of representation confronts the "linear format (that) allows the researcher to demonstrate to professional colleagues the 'objective' nature of the findings, the

---

THEORY INTO ACTION

Time needed: Present the collage project a few weeks in advance. Participants need time to think about it, gather materials, and assemble their creations. Provide 5–10 minutes per person for presenting their collage to the group.

Materials: Most materials will be provided by the participants themselves. As the outline below indicates, collage art can be made of practically anything.

precise conditions under which they were ascertained, and therefore the context of their utility" (Barone, 2000, p. 213).

This collage experience is designed specifically to follow the experiences of building the bubble, the catapults, and composition work for definitive reasons. By now, teachers have developed a sense of how representation, recombination, and reve(a)lation are aesthetically influenced (through space and movement), and how each can shape how we imagine our profession differently. The collage work is slightly more individualized than the preceding experiences. But my goal is for participants to take what new knowledges and aesthetic sensibilities they have acquired up until now into their collage-making process.

The first thing I articulate to the teachers with whom I do this work is that collage art goes well beyond "the poster board," and in fact I encourage them to avoid using poster boards altogether. Sometimes I discuss ahead of the collage making process, for those who may feel overwhelmed or stymied by such an open-ended task, to begin thinking about a metaphor they might use to symbolize what they believe about education. I suggest they explore the artistic ways that their own personal story could be "drawn onto" that metaphoric frame. Common/frequent metaphors for education include, on the negative side: boxes, mazes, prisons, roller coasters or traps; and, on the positive side: flowers, gardens, trees, roads, and quilts. Sometimes simply a basic shape—that is, choosing a cube, a spiral, or a sphere—can symbolize one's views about education and life.

The goal of this art activity is to reassemble pieces from both one's own life and educational experiences/practices to create connections between self-reflection and pedagogy. One outcome of this process is to creatively explore how, as individuals, we impact others—including how, what, and whom we teach, as well as how we design and implement the curricula. This collage experience is most meaningful when it has been built on the preceding activities. It builds upon all of teachers' prior community (and trust) building, as well as other central learning and experiential concepts of play, emergence, serendipity, relationality, and synchronicity. Each of these concepts is necessary for meaningful collage processes and presentations to evolve.

My two rules are always: (1) that it is made of something that can be carried in and out of the building, and (2) it does not violate any building health codes. This second rule is offered partially in jest, yet over the many years I have done this process with both preservice and classroom teachers, I have seen everything including potted plants, a red wagon filled with red wax, a crocheted scarf and hat, musical performances, and video/movies.

I review with teachers the creative concepts such as recycling as transformation. For example, what everyday objects might be lying around (like Maggie's burned piano in *Northern Exposure*—see Chapter 2) that could be transformed into part of their collage? I invite them to think, as they did in composition work (see Chapter 3), and in building the bubble (see Chapter 1), about going above and beyond the flat poster board surface and think about qualities such as levels of space, dimensionality, repetition, alternative uses of materials, and ways that this process might indeed be collaborative even if the collage itself is autobiographical.

The outline for the collage experience when I assign this experience as part of my graduate course for teachers is as follows:

"BEFORE YOU TEACH THE CONTENT, YOU TEACH WHO YOU ARE" (CAHAN & KOCUR, 2000)

The Collage

The goal of this art activity is to reassemble pieces from both your own life and educational experiences/practices to create connections between self-reflection and pedagogy. One of the aims of this class is dealing with how we as individuals impact others—how and what and who we teach as well as how we design and implement the curricula. How does autobiography shape our curriculum theory and how we teach? How do the arts play a role in who you *are* and who you might become? You will be constructing a collage made of various materials and mediums. These materials should include "fragments" from your own history—photos, school work, yearbooks, awards...anything! Also consider images from magazines, newspapers, your own illustrations, "scraps" of other material items. I also encourage you to play with the notion of a frame for your artwork. It does NOT have to be square nor only two-dimensional—think boxes, frames, or other objects aside from poster board to use! Feel free to use any artistic mediums you would like such as paint, crayons, markers, glitter, glue, ribbons, construction paper—the list IS endless!

The Essay

In addition to the collage itself you will write a four- to five-page paper in response to the following prompts divided in two sections:

Collage Process

In what ways did collaging together pieces of your personal schooling history connect your present/future philosophy of teaching and learning?

Reflect on what the *process* of creating your artwork was like. Summarize reactions/thoughts/ideas/questions that emerged as the result of this activity. What was created? What was revealed?

What did you put in your collage and why? How did you decide what to put where? Are there any relationships between things on your collage?

PERSONAL THEORY INTO PRACTICE:

- What is your personal curriculum theory as it relates to the arts?
- What are its roots?
- What social, political and cultural values inform your curriculum theory? Give examples.
- What events, persons, and circumstances helped to shape it?
- What changes do you propose for yourself to further the aims of your curriculum and instructional processes resulting from new insights and understandings?

Here are some examples of collages that have been created over the years, followed by excerpts from the collage-process essay written by the teachers who made them.[3]

Collage Example 1: Marty K (2011)

Marty K: Collecting pieces of my life, picking up the pieces, spreading them in front of me, picking and choosing which I will include in my autobiographical collage, and then the format.... How do you capture a life? Several thoughts occurred to me while completing and working on this assignment: I am not the person in the early photographs, I transformed into an adult, morphed, changed, became a mixture of my life's experiences. It gave me pause when I think of my own classroom full of 10-year-old faces looking up at me. How much of a difference is the school curriculum going to make on them? How much difference am I going to make?... I did not know how to present my collage, the format itself. My initial idea was to wear it. I thought I would put it on a sweat shirt, somehow, and as a symbol of how life grows on you, just simply wear it. I abandoned that idea, started to think about boxes, putting ideas and images in boxes, but as I went through the boxes in my house looking for pictures and other artifacts, it occurred to me I have too many boxes in my house . . . sigh. So, I made a book. It's an exploding book, to symbolize the way you learn when you are young, learn when you are in high school, learn when you are in college and then, as life takes you through her journey, it seems that this information is somehow all inside you and explodes into knew knowledge that you did not expect. When new knowledge enters your brain, it adds in, sometimes multiplies, or even exponentially reacts with all the knowledge that's already in there to create imagination and new thinking. The knowledge that adds in is usually factual, the knowledge that multiplies in could be new ideas that click and make old ideas make more sense, the knowledge that creates exponential growth is knowledge gained through deep understanding often brought about by deep thinking. How's that for a metaphor?

Collage Sample 2: Keri C., 2010, Level I of two levels.

Keri C.: Theory, process, spiral—lots of spirals that glisten because it is my job to send those spirals off to make their mark.... Spiral. Opaque, incandescent, no...reflection, definitely reflection...I'll use mirrors!! Mrs. P., differentiation and Greek Mythology. My perfect room...fluid, serene...yet somehow refreshingly chaotic—upside down, that is it...always reflecting, always going back. My room will be upside down to represent the chaos, and be reflected back off of the mirror on the bottom—symbolizing the place I go to refuel, the place that is my infrastructure, the place that bears the joy, and intellect that I bring to my class—my curriculum. Spirals could actually go either way—up or down—always looking forward, but always able to refuel from the reflections of the past. I have decided to put my spirals at the top. The student is now the teacher, but the teacher must always remain the student.... Dr. B.—you are your past, you are your heritage, you are your choices, you are a picture of stamina, you are light...you are your dreams. This is where my tea lights come in to play. They represent inner light, inner beauty, an eternal flame that is not only living and breathing in me, but one that I am able to pass on. That just answered the question of how to anchor my spirals. My spirals will be anchored in my eternal flame. I love dreaming, for me, I feel as though it is a gift from God that is my personal way of healing, thinking, and discovering. I dream in volumes, able to wake up, go back to sleep and pick up where I left off. I dream in color, and in detail. My teaching—my theory—colorful, and in detail—that is my spiral. Curriculum that is as fluid, joyous, bountiful, intellectual, and revolutionary as life is itself, as the events and people that we call friends, family, and heroes . . . The effects of current social, political and cultural beliefs bend and redefine the shape of curriculum because any teacher worth her weight is redefining her curriculum according to that child in her class. The effect of this dance then spirals to the next generation.

Collage Sample 2: Keri C., 2010, Level II of two levels.

Since I have witnessed this collage experience with teachers most often during our formal Lesley University class, teachers as participants also complete final course evaluations. In this final class evaluation the assignment cited most frequently as being "most valuable" in the class has been the collage. One teacher wrote, "Collage was very beneficial to help me articulate my own curriculum theory," while another expressed, "Learning that who I am as a person does impact my classroom and I need to explore self-identity so that I may honor the nobility in my own students and adjust curriculum to fit their needs."

In my experience, this is the most powerful of all the activities. It is the one that participants often say changes them the most. Many individuals cry tears of sadness or joy as they share their collages with the group. Each collage is inherently personal and autobiographical, and yet equally social and political. Even before completing the process and presenting her collage to the group one teacher emailed me and said: *I've got to tell you that the collage assignment is really an eye-opener. I've always figured that my outside-of-the-classroom experiences were significant, but when as I settled into choosing exactly what to include in the collage . . . wow, even I was surprised.*

Through a critical self-exploration using aesthetic guideposts of recombination, representation and re(veal)ation teachers might produce dangerous knowledge, and dangerous style, that challenge preexisting assumptions about education. By connecting various layers of their own identities within larger world contexts, educators can transform their own future classrooms into sites of democracy and social empowerment.

Notes

1. Jessica is a self-selected pseudonym selected by the study participant.
2. Midwest is a pseudonym for the university Jessica was attending and where I was conducting my dissertation research.
3. Pseudonyms have been given to teachers/teacher work in this book.

SELF, CURRICULUM, AND COLLAGE WORKPAGE

Questions to consider and discuss during and following the completion of the Collage experience. These questions are meant for introspection as well as large group discussions:

1. In what ways did collaging together pieces of your personal schooling history connect you're your present/future philosophy of teaching and learning?

2. Reflect on what the *process* of creating your artwork was like. Summarize reactions/thoughts/ideas/questions that emerged as the result of this activity. What was created? What was revealed? How did creating the artwork impact your memories of childhood? Did it change what you remembered?

3. Describe your artwork—the contents (what you put in your collage and why). How did you decide what to put and where? Does the location of any one piece affect its meaning because of its aesthetic placement *in relation* to other pieces of the collage?

4. What is your personal curriculum theory as it relates to the arts?

5. What social, political, and cultural values inform your curriculum theory?

6. What events, persons, and circumstances helped to shape it?

7. What changes do you propose for yourself to further the aims of your curriculum and instructional processes resulting from new insights and understandings?

5

Left-Handed Curriculum and Social Activism

We map the world, including our moral obligation, through the imagination.
—Rethorst, 1997, p. 3

Theory

Jumping in where the collage experience left off, and having critically reflected on and reexamined the shifting and fluid understandings of self as a relational process, educators begin looking beyond their identities as solely part of the in-school curriculum and look outward toward a more *public* understanding of pedagogy.

This chapter presents a "dolls in a box" project performed in the summer of 2011. The purpose of this project was twofold: (1) to bring educators participation more fully into the realm of the collective/community, and (2) to bring educators into an in-between space that crosses borders and boundaries not only between self and other, but between public policy, public perception, and public personae.

The Left Handed Curriculum, pages 91–101
Copyright © 2013 by Information Age Publishing

Teaching is a political act. Oftentimes I hear educators say that they stay out of "politics," or that education should remain "neutral." It is my belief, supported by the work of Freire (1970/2000), Dewey (1916), McLaren (1998) and others, that education is never neutral. Our everyday classroom decisions and our curricula are both shaped by innumerable factors that go well beyond childhood development theory (see Part I section on defining curriculum for more). According to Jane Turner (2010) with the British Columbia Teachers Federation: "Every time curriculum revisions are contemplated, interest and lobby groups line up at the government's door trying to ensure their perspective is included. Why do they do this? Because what is taught and how it's taught matters" (n.p.). I wonder, what can creativity offer to teachers who wish to disrupt or transform public discourse around teaching and education?

At this juncture in the "left-handed" creative process, teachers are encouraged to find their *public* (and political) voice through artistic means. It is in this next experience that participating educators can explore how creative expression can inform empowered and emancipatory practices in public spaces. In the example shown in this chapter, public placement of teacher and student "dolls in boxes" were employed to dismantle the dominant narrative around education. These efforts inspire community-based collective actions. They remind us that creativity can be a form of protest. As I write in Burdick, Sandlin, and O'Mally's *Problematizing Public Pedagogy* (in press):

> Following in tandem with public and grass roots form of community protest, the art world embraces notions of public pedagogy- arguing for "relational art turned toward explicitly fostering 'socially transformative' art that would incite debate and give participants agency" (Luse, 2010, n.p.). In promoting stronger relationships between public perception and personal (real lived) classroom experiences by teachers, creative artful expressions may convey what words cannot. In the visual arts, an image may, in mere seconds of being viewed, speak what must be written in volumes. (McDermott, in press)

Now more than ever, teacher voices are being silenced. Fear of repercussions, real or imagined, has had a detrimental effect on many educators' right to speak out, to challenge, to question, or even to defend themselves against the onslaught of attacks against their profession. In the current reform climate of high-stakes testing, merit pay, one-size-fits-all curriculum, and legislation across numerous states to eliminate public schools and displace professional educators with a privatized charter school model, this fact is truer than ever. Yet the public spaces for teachers to speak out are minimal. Many fear for their jobs if they resist or oppose the fear-based, top-down approach being launched in their schools. The public face of educators is under severe attack. The arts can become a way for educators to become activists without using their words. They might show what cannot be said.

While dominant narratives around teacher "accountability" are themselves a form of public pedagogy—one that enforces restrictions and sanctions as educational "necessities," O'Malley (2006, in Sandlin, O'Mally & Burdick, 2011), in contrast, calls for a "public pedagogy of *possibility*," which "dissents from and disrupts the standardization worldview itself, understanding that standardization of curriculum and assessment is but one consequence of a larger social paradigm" (p. 339).

In an effort to reclaim the public narrative around education, teachers and parents must go beyond writing letters to the editor and petitions. While I believe these efforts to be worthwhile they are only half the battle. Public space is frequently a visual embodied landscape. As explored in Chapter 1, the curriculum as a "public moral enterprise" (Gatzambide-Fernandez & Sears, 2004) must convey messages through all of our senses in the spaces which we inhabit, and not merely our two-dimensional intellectual thinking. The notion that curriculum itself is a public act has been explored by many scholars (Gaztambide-Fernandez, 2004; Luse, 2010); Sandlin, O'Mally, & Burdick, 2011), and if art is an embodied element *within* curriculum, then it follows that it too involves various modes of relationality between what is considered private and that which is considered public through aesthetic engagements. I hope that such artistic engagements might elevate teachers' sense of (private) self and (public) voice to the level of "official knowledge," and holding their own voices to the same status. I hope that publicly engaging art will encourage teachers to speak out more when provided with the public venues to honor their "private" thoughts. I hope that the equation: private = public = political artistic practices with educators will bear witness to the power of collective action when many small private voices can speak out as one.

THEORY INTO ACTION

Time: From 30 minutes to several hours.

Materials: soft cloth materials (bed sheets work well); doll stuffing such as batting, though recyclable plastic grocery bags are cheaper and "greener"; glue guns, yarn, markers, and other decorative embellishments.

Willinsky (2006) calls us to the task of encouraging educators to see themselves as public intellectuals in arguing that by making their work public, teachers might better envision themselves as curriculum leaders in which their standing as public (and moral) intellectuals can be enacted through the arts. So to this end I developed a project aimed at giving teachers "voice" through the arts.

The Out of the Box Doll Project is a way to merge two key ideas into practice: (1) that teachers can use aesthetics to critically engage in educational discourse, and (2) that critical aesthetics in education can and should become an act of public pedagogy—voiced by teachers in public spaces. The origin of this project has its roots in the Save Our Schools march on Washington (www.saveourschoolsmarch.org) held in July 2010 in Washington, DC. As part of that movement I invited teachers to make doll figures of themselves to be placed in boxes and brought to the steps of the Department of Education. Earlier that same month, I had attended the Free Minds, Free People conference, where I had a doll-making station and invited teachers and students to make a doll of themselves while I explained how and where these dolls were to be presented. By the end of the conference I had sixty dolls. There were three basic objectives for this action: break teacher silence, change the public narrative, and create acts of visual dissent.

Break the Silence

Teachers have been silenced. Their right to dissent has been stifled through coercive fear-based tactics. While many wish to protest current policy reform measures, they often cannot do so directly without professional repercussions.

Change the Public Narrative

"Reform" policymakers have a stranglehold on the current narrative surrounding education. The corporate agenda for public education in the forms of high-stakes testing, school vouchers, and for-profit charter schools rely on framing the public perception based on assumptions and stereotypes such as: (1) schools are in crisis (see *A Nation at Risk*, 1983; *Waiting for Superman*, 2010), and (2) bad teachers are to blame. The film *Waiting for Superman* (2010) has become the iconic stereotype of teachers who are "lazy" and schools that are "failing." The framing around this public narrative now invites new legislation that enforces greater restrictions and sanctions upon both teachers and students for failure to comply with the new rules.

Create a Visual Landscape of Dissent

What teachers cannot say, they can still display. Public placement of teacher and student dolls in boxes can help dismantle the dominant narrative. They inspire community-based collective actions. They remind us that creativity can be a form of protest. In accordance with Reinsborough and Cannine (2010), I contend that "'show me don't tell me' means that the story's meaning or moral is shown to us rather than told to us" (p. 39). They add that "effective stories communicate by connecting to what people already know and hold dear—our values. When a story is showing, instead of telling, it offers the audience the opportunity to use their own values and draw conclusions" (p. 39).

"Speaking truth to power, truth to policy." Fifty teacher dolls in boxes in front of the U.S. Department of Education in Washington DC, July 2011.

Here is the original project description in its entirety:

OUT OF THE BOX DOLL PROJECT

What Is This?

These dolls in boxes have been created by teachers and students from across the country, most of them made at the Free Minds, Free People conference (www.fmfp.org) held in Rhode Island, July 2011. Each doll was made with cloth material (old bed sheets purchased at Goodwill) and cut into a body shape designed by the person making it. Each individual then created the personal features; sometimes hair, face and eyes, while others chose to write a personal message on their doll. The seams were closed using a hot glue gun and stuffed with newspapers, plastic grocery bags, or scrap cloth.

Why Are They Here?

The purpose of this event is to call attention to educators, students, parents and community members who have been facing increasing restrictions on their rights to a meaningful and democratic education due to policies over the last ten years going back to No Child Left Behind, and more currently Race to the Top.

While it is students, teachers, and parents who have the greatest stake in the decisions being made in educational policy, they have the least voice and visibility. The purpose of the Out of the Box Doll project is to create a *visible public space* for these grass-roots stakeholders, usually marginalized from the decision making, to be seen and heard. The dolls in boxes are a visual representation of a collective stand in opposition to the practices of "boxing in" students and teachers in the name of accountability and at the expense of creative, meaningful, and sustainable educational practices. The makers of these dolls are committed to transforming the "boxed in" approach to education into creative and innovative spaces for meaningful learning to occur.

Now is the time to make our opposition to restrictive educational policies that reduce teachers to technicians and student to a product. We need to make our voices heard and our faces visible so that policy makers know that we are many in this opposition! We support creative, student-centered, and meaningful learning for all students. Our dolls in boxes are a demonstration of our collective commitment to supporting teachers and our children. Public education is more than teaching to a test, and delivering information handed down from textbook companies. It is our democratic right to a public education that supports democratic values.

The dolls in boxes surrounding the steps of the Department of Education garnered some attention[1] and provided an inroad for two of the Save Our Schools organizers (Bess Altwerger and Rick Meyer) and myself to meet with Secretary of Education Arne Duncan who himself received a doll in a box made by me personally to give to him. (Note to readers: If you want to tell the educational administration how *you* feel about education—make them a doll in a box. Apparently it gets their attention.)

Doll in Box, made for Secretary of Education, Arne Duncan.

I also created a Facebook page following the course of events, and inviting teachers from all over the country to create their "out of the box" movements in their communities. On this page I wrote:

> We encourage individuals and groups from everywhere to begin their own "Out of the Box" initiatives. Make dolls and place them around your community and schools! Let it be known publicly and visibly that teachers, educators, and parents from across the country support a public education that promotes teacher professionalism, student-driven curriculum, and the importance of creative engagement to promote meaningful learning in the classroom. Post your dolls on this Facebook site so that we can share our visions for change with each other.

One person who commented on the Facebook page responded, "Thank you so much for your work with this project! I look forward to making my doll and taking this back to my community! :)"

How to Make a Teacher-Doll

Lay two pieces of fabric[2] one on top of the other and trace out a human shape figure approximately two to three feet high. Use markers and paints to create a face, clothes, and words on the front side of the doll (or to decorate however you choose). Using a glue gun, seal the seams between the two layers around the edges, leaving fist-wide spaces at the top and bottom for stuffing. Stuff the doll with preferred material and glue the openings shut. When the doll is finished and the personal message conveying how you refuse to be "boxed in" has been completed, place the doll (and message if separate from the doll) in a cardboard box and place in designated public space.

Doll in box, made at the Free Minds, Free People conference, July, 2011.

Dolls made at Free Minds, Free People conference, July, 2011.

Reflections on the Possibilities for the Project

Sometimes it feels less risky to express oneself through a vehicle that is one step removed from pen or mouth. Not too unlike dolls used by counselors to help children explore difficult issues or trauma, by writing their messages (oftentimes anonymously) on the dolls, the dolls seem to be able to "say" what many teachers feel they cannot. This aesthetic gesture brings teachers closer to bridging the divide between the isolation of their classrooms and the public sphere where so many of the decisions made about educational policy are sold to our society. I believe that by using the Out of the Box Doll Project, teachers can make "sense of their experiences individually, but also jointly negotiated larger meanings and developed public spaces in which to practice lived experiences" (Wilson, 2000, p. 41). *The Encyclopedia of Activism and Social Justice* states:

> By the 1990's, do-it-yourself (DIY) avant-garde agitational groups sought to break down the lines between art and life and introduce creativity, imagination, play, and pleasure into activism.... As public spaces [are] transformed within this burlesque of do-it-yourself protest, creative play [is] recognized as an effective approach. What links these protest gestures is an appreciation for the transformative possibilities of creative play. (p. 314)

Creative change in curriculum is personal, as explored in many of the other experiences in previous chapters. Yet so much of curriculum is equally political, and it is in this arena that teachers' voices are often muted. Creativity takes courage on so many levels. Many educators become nervous even being asked to draw pictures, as in Chapter 1, feeling a sense of self-consciousness about their artistic abilities, sometimes hovering somewhere around "stick figures." Fear can be a powerful silencing agent. The ultimate goal of the experiences in this book is not to help teachers build their courage to become creative beings, but to use their creativity to become courageous beings. I am reminded of the words of Ayers (2004), who writes, "Education ignites new ways of seeing the world and so the fundamental message of the teacher begins with the belief that you can change your life. As this evolves, a necessary corollary emerges: transformed, you must change the world" (p. 160).

Notes

1. For more news coverage on this event also see http://blogs.edweek.org/edweek/campaign-k12/2011/07/duncan_meets_with_school_march.html and http://blogs.edweek.org/edweek/campaign-k-12/2011/07/today_kicks_off_the_four-day.html

2. Note about the fabric choices: It was brought to my attention at another doll-making session at the 11th Annual Curriculum and Pedagogy Conference in October 2011 that perhaps fabric colors, rather than being flowered, striped, blue, purple or green for example, should more accurately reflect real skin colors of a diverse people. Taking this observation to heart, I suggest that it may be too easy to "default" to white or light colored fabric because it's easier to write on. It is important to avoid having vast numbers of teacher dolls that end up representing merely one racially homogenous and dominant group. My feeling is that the fabric choices reflect cultural and racial diversity, and color choices should be based on the cultural and aesthetic consensus of the group making the dolls. Darker fabrics work well with white chalk and other light paints for writing/decorating.

LEFT-HANDED CURRICULUM AND SOCIAL ACTIVISM WORKPAGE

After reading Chapter 5, discuss as a group the following questions and set up time and dates to take action!

1. What assumptions and stereotypes about teachers are prevalent in the current dominant public narrative? What stories about schools, teachers, and public education do you see in the major media news outlets? What stereotypes confound teachers' public image even further in pop culture such as film and television?

2. What personal and collective truths about teachers, teaching, and education do you feel are being silenced by the media, and why? What would *you* like to say if given the chance?

3. Think about artful ways you (as a group) could create powerful images or creative actions that could be publicly viewed (such as the Dolls in Boxes project) that speak to your answers in question #2. Draw from what you've learned so far about the role(s) that aesthetics play in provoking emotion, eliciting reactions, and "telling" by "showing."

4. Generate a list of concerns (fears, repercussions) and of assets (what will be gained by this action). Strategize! Then, make a concrete plan to make it happen—nothing "out there" will ever change by simply thinking about it!

6

The Journey Forward

Paint Your Life™

Theory: Where Do We Go From Here?

When I teach the sequence of experiences outlined in Chapters 1–5, in my classes on Curriculum through the Arts, we usually conclude with the collages—as a celebration of who we are as teachers and who we wish to become as creative beings. However, that does not mean that the journey ends there. If you have come this far in the book, I encourage you and your colleagues to journey forward and explore additional pathways to creatively transform your curriculum, your teaching, and your selves. One way to do this is to springboard now into another creative program called *Paint Your Life* (PYL). *PYL* has been internationally recognized for 15 years as a process that enables students, teachers, artists, and business people to reimagine their lives and their world by thinking with images rather than words. As defined by Jacquelyn Thunfors, the program's creator, "*Paint Your Life* TM is a radical fast track to the creative unconscious. For artists, teachers, anyone who secretly knows with the 'right system' their ideas could appear and change our world." Thunfors has brought this program to communities across three continents to the countries of South Africa, Greece, and China.

Like the experiences in this book, *Paint Your Life* involves a set of interlocking artistic processes that are aimed at "unlocking the creative potential" (Thunfors, 2009) in every individual. The *Paint Your Life* program may be completed in one day-long session, or spread out across a two half days, depending on the needs of the group. However, Thunfors recommends completing the games in one day for teachers, principals, and other professionals, as the increasing intensity of the timed and interlocking games is designed to create true brain changes that generate 100% original results for most participants at their level.

I had the good fortune to meet Jacquelyn Thunfors in 2010. I was introduced to her book *Paint Your Life* (2009) first, and seeing the amazing potential in working with teachers, I contacted her immediately. While the *Paint Your Life* program is for anyone and everyone desiring to discover how their own untapped creative potential can change their lives, the potential for educators seemed endless. Following a couple of face-to-face meetings and phone calls, she and I arranged (with a grant from my institution—Towson University) for her to come to Maryland and conduct the workshop specifically with a group of educators from Howard County Schools. Their experience with this program will be shared in the "Action" section of this chapter. But first, what is *Paint Your Life*, and why do I include it as part of this book?

Chapters 1–5 of this book help encourage educators to think through their senses, through the aesthetics of the world around us, and through the media of different art forms—to reexamine the power of curriculum as a creative domain. *Paint Your Life* draws participants more deeply into their own intuitive and internal processes, a journey "without words" (Thunfors, 2009), through the use of visual mixed-media such as pastels, pencils, or other dry color medium on paper. Following the completion of the journey taken in Chapters 1–5, I believe educators are primed to explore their inner potential using a specific art experiences developed in *PYL*. It is the next ideal movement forward in the creative left-handed journey.

Why Is The Paint Your Life Experience Vital to Schools?

The rising tide of standardized education in the U.S., and a one-size-fits-all model of measurement, is rapidly dissolving our innate power as professional educators to create meaningful life-changing experiences in our classrooms. To combat this dilemma, the internationally renowned and well proven *Paint Your Life* creative "game" system takes teachers and administrators through a sequential and interlocking series of structured and personalized artistic experiences, which are by now 100% successful in empowering educators to discover their own, often well-hidden, aptitudes. It immediately enables teachers to conceive ways to take their transformative *PYL* experience into their classrooms, as well as into their own lives. Teacher-participants from around the world have shared the following about their *PYL* experiences:

> You opened a creative door to things I have never thought of before- a whole new dimension. So many of your ideas I have passed on to my students. Like a stone in a pond your ideas just ripple. You open up the abilities we had as a child and lost. (Angela Burns, artist and art educator, Connecticut)
>
> Your workshop allowed my soul to dance again. I felt a connectivity to my inner being, a place I had long forgotten about. The workshop was life changing. (Shawn Dunn, lawyer, teacher, community coordinator for Marion Ridge, Pinetown, South Africa)

Ideally, the initial impulse and motivation to *be* a teacher, to transfer skills and ideas to others, should be based upon one's own self-confidence and joy in experimenting in the world of ideas on your own. Using the *PYL* system, one learns quickly that hidden aptitudes in oneself and others are the norm, not the exception. "The potential for many careers, in a long lifetime, lies within the head of nearly every human being" (Thunfors, 2009, p. 10).

According to *Phi Beta Kappa* editor John Churchill (2010), education today does not adequately prepare students for unpredictable careers and unknown futures. As a teacher, you should not only know this but experience it before taking on the crucial experiences you must generate, usually alone, within your classroom. *Paint Your Life* unlocks and generates the joy of discovery—the element most lacking in standardized U.S. curricula, on both sides of the learning equation—student and teacher.

The goals of the *PYL* system, as an essential new training ground for educators, are to enable teachers to:

1. Truly enjoy exploring creative differentiation strategies in all your classrooms. Exposing differentiation strategies to your students provides the best result surprises.
2. Celebrate the fascinating intellectual complexity that culturally inclusive classrooms provide. Higher levels of personal growth and student growth are consistently generated by the *PYL* system.
3. Develop problem-based authentic lessons and assessments. Via their *PYL* insights, these become a joy to construct and implement in your classroom.

Like the experiences in the previous chapters, no artistic experience is required to complete the *PYL* program. Those previously trained in the arts usually discover, via the *Paint Your Life* games, that they have lost many years of *creative flow* working on a poorly selected singular wavelength—a wavelength that limited their own potential and made them the unsuspecting victim of specialization. Educators too can *conceive new visions* for their own professional goals. When evaluating students whose performance challenges the norm, educators find themselves *considering entirely new points of view.*

THEORY INTO ACTION

Time: The PYL workshop requires approximately eight hours to complete the interlocking system of creative experiences, and to complete a debriefing/discussion session. The workshop may be held during one full day or may be broken up into two or three (4) hour sessions.

Materials: Two books are required of all participants—*Journalist Without Words: 19 Years Painting International Conversations* (2007) and *Paint Your Life* (Thunfors, 2009).[1] Other materials include large rolls of plain white paper; dry media such as pastels, chalk, and colored pencils; tape; easels; and 8 × 10 pieces of paper for each participant. The ideal space for this program includes a lot of natural light, windows, and space for movement.

While the *PYL* program is available to anyone interested in creatively changing their lives, Thunfors advocates that the program be led by a trained *Paint Your Life* facilitator.[2] A facilitator, deeply familiar with the process and attuned to creative group dynamics, may guide a group with thought-provoking questions and appropriate pacing. According to Thunfors, under the guidance of a trained *PYL* facilitator, a group may experience the following benefits:

- Time spent on each interlocking game is allocated and compressed, not only according to the game itself, but according to the unique pace of participants themselves. Acceleration improves response in most cases.
- The atmosphere is arranged, changed, and adjusted continuously in direct rhythm to each game and its participants.
- The hidden algorithm of the group is activated. Those self-confidently risking conceptual fluidity often animate their neighbors, whose wisdom traditionally emanates in words, not shapes.

- Each person receives individual game to game support and nourishment. As mindsets unpeel, energy flags and soars, dips, flares, often roars ahead of the hand.
- It is recognized that comparative motivational insights are the norm. Experienced *PYL* moderators share insights from many other cultural norms and often document professional breakthroughs and recognize and define standard motivational blocks.
- There is assurance that the joy of the mutual "group search" enthusiasm spreads consistently higher with each "completion–startup again" sequence. Team joy evolves and carries each person through their own singular and limited mindset ("limited" meaning the unspoken agony of each of us, stranded in this world with only one brain, one set of experiences to lean on.)
- Ensures thoughts processed through the "timed-group funnel" can help trump singular leisurely thought—the "bounce effect." Many professionals, in many disciplines, have never experienced this invisible force vector, vis-à-vis singular brain power. Specialization can often wither latent brain channels.
- Empathy dominates. A Greek chorus, all your own, swells and swells as the papers pile up around your ankles, the day progressing toward its unique norm.
- Group members are guided to offer advice and suggestions to each fellow participant at the end of the day (for those who wish guidance or response) according to their own wisdom and applicable experience.

The moderator takes responsibility for summation of achievements of the group, as well as offers personalized guidance and recommendations for each participant, if requested.

A Brief Outline of the Activities and Sample Work

> *Looking at things differently through art changed me.*
> —Howard County teacher participant

The rich and complex nature of each of these activities is beyond the scope of this chapter. I recommended that you get a copy of *Paint Your Life* (Thunfors, 2009) for a full exploration of each of these activities with the full descriptions they deserve. However, a "snapshot" of each one is briefly discussed here, including examples from the teacher workshop in Howard

County, MD in 2010. In this workshop, the group engaged with the first six of the eight *PYL* games.

Game One: In Transito

In keeping with one of the central themes running through this book, *emergence*, Thunfors (2009) writes, "All art is perishable. Ink runs. Oil paint cracks. Glue weakens and discolors. Acid eats. Canvas punctures. Glass breaks. Heat melts. Cold cracks. Moisture opens. Worms eat. Color fades" (p. 15). This aesthetically inspired reminder of the transitory nature of life itself speaks to Chris' statement in *Northern Exposure*[3] that, "what I'm dealing with is the aesthetics of the transitory. I'm creating tomorrow's memories—and as memories my images are as immortal as art." Such words remind us that curriculum is not a thing, but rather a process, and it is in and through the process that we inspire learners and ourselves. True learning rests not with test scores but with the memories we create, which students may carry into a meaningful adult life.

In this first game, participants are asked to create a work of art on an envelope to mail/give to someone special to them. According to Thunfors (2009):

> More valuable than the result is training your eye to vision a design in a very small space. Also, the unseen space—the backside—will begin sparking you for attention, maybe stimulating you to compose an ideation that moves both eye and mind to the reverse space, doubling the challenge, doubling the potential. (p. 16)

In Transito, oil pastels on envelope, Howard County, MD *PYL* workshop, 2010.

One participant reflected after the workshop:

> I could see the envelope activity being the most useful in one's personal life. I gave the envelope to my mom and she was so excited! She asked what the purpose of the activity was. When I explained it to her, she inquired about hers. It was a nice way to lead into a personal discussion. It was very rewarding. It also took me back to my childhood. I gave my mom my artwork and she complemented me just like she did when I was young. I even asked her if it was going to go on the refrigerator!

Readers who have undergone the experience outlined in Chapter 1: Curriculum as Space might revisit and deepen their awareness of space as curriculum, playing on Thunfors' words. What spaces are left unseen that emit tremendous potential in our classrooms? How can retraining the eye and the imagination to see these spaces differently transform our pedagogy?

Game Two and Game Five: Time Freeze/Visual Personality

This begins as a list generated by each of the participants (to be used in a later activity), in which everyone names their 26 "favorite" things such as favorite ice cream, favorite movie, artist, and architectural style in an interview with a fellow participant. This outline becomes an illustrated version of each participant's life. "No one will ever be you. No one will ever replicate the precise personae you have constructed and become. Only you can become its visual architect" (Thunfors, 2009, p. 19). Toward the end of the workshop, in Game Five, participants swap lists and using the 26 clues, everyone creates an illustration of that other person, drawing their life on paper for them to see. The final product becomes a collage of sorts, one that shares who we are as unique individuals. Working from Chapter 4: Self, Curriculum, and Collage, this process deepens our relational nature to one another. Rather than visually constructing one's *own* collage, the process of having *someone else* depict for another person their interpretation of how to symbolically reassemble the items of the list reminds us how much we are each our own selves, and yet our identity is equally contingent upon how others choose to construct our identities for us. Such a process enriches our capacity for self-reflection and celebration of each other.

It also reminds us that curriculum ought not to be a one-size-fits-all model for instruction. Imagine the students in classrooms, combined with the knowledges and skill sets that are important, each as unique combinations within their own socio-geographical and historical moments. As Thunfors says, "There is no one pattern for this except the one you devise. Each person chooses different items from their list than others probably would. Some items seem useless and are. There are no rules" (2009, p. 32).

Visual Personality is an aesthetic reminder that all knowledges and meaning-making are co-constructed processes that involve students, teachers, and various facets of our collective or individual lived experiences. The guiding questions for all educators must remain: What knowledge is worth most, to whom, and to what end?

Visual Personality, colored pastels on paper, Howard County, MD *PYL* workshop, 2010.

One participant wrote in a feedback form following the end of the workshop that:

> The interview and exchange with someone to look at and think about and then create a poster about the person, with sharing time [was the most delightful aspect of the workshop].

Game Three: Inside-Out
Using a large (28" × 32") piece of white or light brown roll paper taped to a hard surface such as an easel or cardboard, participants are asked to

"explore" their workshop space, going outdoors or by large windows where they can find spaces that juxtapose an inside space with an outside space. As Thunfors (2009) states, "You are looking for an inspirational scene, inside to out, or outside to in, that enables you to give an unusual new experience to the person who sees this spatially innovative drawing" (p. 25).

Black pastel on paper, Howard County, MD *PYL* workshop, 2010.

This game is about taking and retaking on our notions of perspective. As stated in the Introduction to this book, education is never neutral. Like all other human phenomena, education re-entrenches, situates, or liberates our positionality. What we "see" or how we make meaning is always related to the position from which we stand. The same is true of our students. How often do they see the traditional textbook curriculum from the "outside" looking "in" and feel alienated from the content therein? As the song "Acknowledge Your Own History" (1989) by the music group Jungle Brothers says: "Page one, page two, page three . . . and still no sign of me." How can we alter the positionality of the content and processes of our curriculum so that students may stand in *different* (and more meaningful) relationships to the knowledge and experiences we intend to impart? In essence this speaks to the juxtaposition of the *Curriculum of the Eye/I* (McDermott, 2011)—what we see and who we are as intrinsically related.

Game Four: Boat Dancing

Using a large piece of roll paper and object to draw on, as in Game Four, participants will select three colors of their choosing and identify an object/space to draw. Sitting comfortably, the person keeps their eyes focused on the thing to be drawn, and commits to *not* looking at the paper upon which they are drawing. Using their "mind's-eye," the individual draws what they see, three times, each time with a different color (never lifting their hand off the page nor looking at the drawing itself until it's completed). Such a process requires a great deal of *faith* in the process and *trust* in oneself—two elements sorely lacking in today's education reform climate. In explaining this game, Thunfors (2009) tells her readers, "Without probably being aware of it, your brain has become a vast onion-layered globe of experience . . . today you are going to train yourself to lean completely on that great unknown inside onion" (p. 39).

An exercise such as this is the embodiment of a left-handed curriculum—one that requires "leaning on the instinct and eye, alone" which "usually proves unbearable at first" because such action is "over-the-top and risky" (Thunfors, 2009, p. 41). Remember, at the beginning of this book I shared how practicing a left-handed curriculum requires "dangerous style."

Boat Dancing, pastel on paper, from Howard County, MD PYL workshop, 2010.

As such, "the design appears without your knowledge. Your left brain has dozed while your hand flew around what you saw" (Thunfors, 2009, p. 41). As a result, participants discover a completely unique and fascinating work of art with many layers and shapes before them, that they created without forcing their logical brain to place things in "the right order."

How does *Boat Dancing* create a "dangerous style" for enacting curriculum? I remind teachers often that our goal is to teach students, not curriculum. How often do we as teachers focus so much on the written curriculum that we lose sight of the students? What if we were to treat the curriculum guides like we did our drawing paper, and focused instead on the object (or people) in front of us, never looking down at the guide but instead using faith and trust as our guides? If we "let go" of proscribed expectations, and allowed our right brain to take over, what inspirational and creative curricular outcomes might result? This again speaks to the idea of the power of emergence in educational practices.

Additionally, many teachers from the Howard County group immediately anticipated how they could use this activity in their classrooms. Following the workshop, participants commented:

- ▪ I really enjoyed the activity with the single line, which we drew three times. It is easy to do, and the quality of the final project is fun and interesting. It appears to be a piece of abstract art, but then when you look closely you can see that it is a picture of a landscape. It is very cool!
- ▪ I like the three crayon idea and I could incorporate that!

Game Six: Outside-In

In Game Six, participants transform the inner self toward relationships with the "outside" world in creative and unexpected ways. The process reminds us that so much of what drives us everyday are in fact those elements of the world which we cannot "see" with our eyes. Thunfors (2009) reminds us, "Most everything around us appears square, straight, cubed, linear. But in actuality we ride on a curving ball of a planet, spinning tipped in space. We know it. We read about it. But we can't actually see it" (p. 47).

In this game, each individual reconnects with the people and experiences that have influenced them the most, drawing on the worlds that we cannot (or can no longer) see. "We also can't," Thunfors adds, "see all the myriad faces of the people who have loved us, taught us, nourished and trained us to be the person we have become" (2009, p. 47).

Pastel on paper, Howard County, MD *PYL* workshop, 2010.

Game Six is an imaginative way to further explore the idea of public pedagogy discussed in Chapter 5 of this book. Like the dolls in boxes, the visual representation of ourselves created in this game speak to the power that our voices can have on the world around us and how the world, and other people, in turn shape who we are and can become. It also reminds us that true education is not merely contained with the four walls of a classroom, but extends to the world beyond the schoolyard. In response to this game, one participant noted:

> I think the last activity that focused on reflecting on life and sketching ideas—looking at people that have made an impact—great way to be thankful for the impact others have had, and a great way to share and get to know others on a deeper level.

Another teacher stated:

> The activity that I was most surprised by was the final activity when we painted our personal lives above and below the curved line. I was surprised how much thought each person put into their artwork and how much feeling was generated with the game. I was also surprised to see how much everyone shared to the group about their personal lives. It was an emotional time for many people, and the group provided a safe environment. I was pleased to see how therapeutic the process was.

Other Responses to the PYL Workshop

Without prompting or direction, many participants from Howard County brought some of these games immediately back to their classrooms and then invited me in to see the work of their students. Such actions suggest the power and effectiveness of these games on positively influencing the sense of creative power generated by the participants. Unfortunately, we did not have time to complete the remaining two PYL games that day, but they can be found in the book *Paint Your Life* (Thunfors, 2009). After the workshop, participants were asked to write their thoughts and feedback. Some of the comments included:

- I was delighted to see so many people open up and share about themselves.
- How much I learned about the other people in the group. [I was] surprised at the intimate sharing of some people in the room who had just met for the first time, enjoyed conversations with sharing, wish there had been more time for that
- What surprised me the most was discovering my artistic ability I never knew I had!
- That I made a picture that was good and I could let others think more about it. I was angry at first to make a drawing about those that I have lost, but it actually gave me peace.
- [I was surprised] at how emotional so many of us became—how deep we went to express ourselves.
- As an educator, I think this would be interesting because so much of our job is to transmit knowledge and ideas to our students. Art would be an interesting way to explore this.

Additionally, teachers were able to articulate how they would bring the *PYL* games back to their classrooms:

- Thanks for organizing, fascinating topic to think about how to unleash the creativity amongst students, and spur on their thinking and analyzing in new ways- I'm excited to try and extend their writing now that they've 'drawn' their interviews, and see if this helps serve as a springboard for their writing about another friend in the class I enjoyed spending the day with fellow teachers with a passion to reach their students . . .
- This county supports the arts! I feel we do a very nice job because I went through this system. We shouldn't be so test driven and I believe exploration impacts learning.

- ▪ Howard County Schools should have this group come together to see how we can make changes in the class and in parents view of the educational system.
- ▪ Great way to share with kids and adults a form of expression-how to express ideas visually.
- ▪ I will use each of these ideas connecting with literature and other subjects.

As to the impact of this innovative *PYL* concept on our educational systems, philosopher Henri Bergson (cited in Thunfors, 2009) said it perfectly: *On ne descend pas dan la riviere le deuxiemme temps* (One never descends into the river twice. Each experience in life changes us and we are never the same as yesterday.) *Paint Your Life* experience, for educators, demonstrates this ancient maxim *in extremis*: Teachers become, overnight, a vital rejuvenating force in the entire U.S. system they represent. In the words of Thunfors (in unpublished communication):

> Like water, via the *Paint Your Life* process, the mind seeks and arrives at its own level. No one that we know has ever devised a genuine system, in the form of group games that makes this happen, under a certified process. It took 15 years to perfect…in 5 cultures…and IF you uncover an artist, educator, or member of your organization that chooses to go on and become certified themselves, your organization will have real feathers in your hat for advancing something that ensures vast changes in education, communities, and businesses alike. (n.d.)

Notes

1. *Journalist Without Words* documents the global establishment of Jacquelyn Thunfors' trademark concept "journalart"-the transmission of ideas without words. *Paint Your Life* is her second trademark, obtained for this PYL innovative game system, which is now in the patent process .Together, the books give participants a unique view of their own distinctive international potential, once they have become PYL graduates.
2. For more information on how to bring a trained PYL facilitator to your community see the Paint Your Life website at http://www.paintyourlife.org/
3. See Chapter 2 for expanded discussion of this theme and quote.

7

Conclusion

Get one generation as the 'tested generation' and we'll have a bunch of educators who cannot effectively imagine an alternative.
—Wayne Au, 2011, p. 75

Desai (2009) suggests that art "has increasingly drawn the attention of educators interested in re-conceptualizing education in these times of testing, standardization, and accountability" (p. 25). Further, she argues that we need to "develop a politics of the imagination in schools and universities that strategically uses the power of the image to 'unframed' the serious issues that we face today by asking critical questions that envision alternative just futures" (p. 25).

What we are gradually losing beneath our feet are the capacities to imagine what teaching and learning *can* look like, and how we might move through education as a democratic and transformative process. It is my hope that the experiences in this book encourage teachers to remember that emergence, collaboration, and transformation have significant value in the curriculum, as well as transforming society.

The Left Handed Curriculum, pages 117–122
Copyright © 2013 by Information Age Publishing

Revisiting Emergence, Collaboration and Transformation

Emergence

Maxine Greene (1995) writes:

> It is a primary purpose of education to deny people the opportunity for feeling bored or for "succumbing to a feeling of futility, or to the belief that they have come to an end of what is worth having." ... [I]t is the imagination—with its capacity to both make order out of chaos and open experience to the mysterious and the strange—that moves us to go on a quest, to journey where we have never been. (p. 23)

How often are we willing to "push the envelope," or to stand at the edge where perhaps we don't already know the terrain? Can we consider the possibility of going where we do not have predetermined answers as our maps, before even beginning the journey? Massey (1995) proclaims that, "with these maps/space you never lose your way, are never surprised by an encounter with something unrelated" (p. 222). Our notions of maintaining control, of operating only with the lights on begs that we dare not go into the unknown. Massey counters fear with hopes that a new space might emerge, one where we could instead "map dislocation, to leave possibilities open" (p. 223). Sometimes we don't know what is going to happen or where a teachable moment in the classroom is going to go. God forbid, it might not even be on the test. The fact that it matters to kids should matter more, don't you think?

Collaboration

Teachers work together. Creativity isn't something a teacher goes into the back room and mixes up in a beaker. It happens through our communities when we share a common vision and look toward our imagination for solutions and then enact them. We must detach our schools and children from the "number thumpers" who want to isolate teachers from one another and promote competition against one another as the model for students and schools. Race to the Top in itself suggests that there must also be losers. Where exactly are we racing toward anyway?

Transformation

The goals of everyday teaching cannot always be predicted on the outcomes or objectives sheet written by someone hundreds of miles away in some office building, working for a textbook company. He or she does not know the unique needs of your individual children and how learning must be creatively accommodated to meet his or her needs. The writer of those scripted objectives does not know your individual communities. The content of what we teach, even if it's standards-driven, *must* reflect the needs and identities of kids and their everyday lived experiences. The meaningful and powerful accommodations needed from day to day, from classroom to classroom, and from child to child do not come in a teacher's guide. They come from creative problem solving on the part of the teacher, with other teachers and the community. They come from being open to imagine what each child needs and how best to create that learning space for them. *It does not come* on a standardized test.

As part of the creative process, a willingness to make this quest is vital for work to be an act of transformation. The works and writing of many postmodern and critical theorist have brought forth images of a world where there is no "one right answer." Their ideas illuminate a more authentic way of carving out a space, a map of "dislocation," for actions and perceptions that are the foundation of a left-handed curriculum. Transformation of self, much less of education or society, is not a painless process. It demands the death of long-held notions and ideals about ourselves and the world. It impacts our values and our practices as scholars or practitioners, and offers us ways to become better human beings. Artistic ways of rendering curriculum "heal" the split between self and other, and between what we believe and what we practice. Instead, "the teacher weaves together a process that works with family names, society's names, and the child's own fictive sense of his or her own possibilities" (Grumet, 1993, p. 206).

Post-avant-garde art transforms. This is because it is distinctively, socially, and critically "action-oriented." Post-avant-garde art embodies transitory, collectively constructed, spontaneous "acts of becoming" that engender action and social change. The experiences discussed in this book are about, as Gablik (1991) calls it, a "'reframing' of our world from one dominated by the paradigm of Cartesian objectivism, individual experience isolated from social context, and non-relational ways of knowing to one that embraces inter-connectedness, active participation and a sense of wholeness" (p. 43).

Just as art "may realize its purpose through relationship or a conscious collaboration with the audience to deal with an ecological or social agenda" (Gablik, 1991, p. 32), so may a left-handed curriculum, using a critical post-avant-garde framework, realize previously unimagined or excluded meanings and possibilities for the future of education.

The primary aim of critical post-avant-garde educational practices is to reexamine ourselves in light of the need for transformative social agency and ecological imperatives. Post-avant-garde art requires us to blur the boundaries between self and other, between human systems and natural systems, to rupture the false dichotomies set into motion during the modernist era, and more recently being promoted through efforts of corporate-run school reform.

Whether you've been in the profession for one year or thirty years, it's easy in the current climate of attack on teachers (which micromanages our every move under the punitive gaze of the microscope) to forget why we are here. We must (re)discover who we are and what we came here to do. Top-down, one-size-fits-all reform measures are put in to place supposedly to prevent "bad teaching" from happening. Yet, with such measures, we no longer simply avoid it, we almost guarantee bad teaching. Teachers need to examine deeply and creatively who they are. For if we cannot know ourselves, or willingly embrace the emergent, fractured, collective, and individual parts of ourselves that are (like art) always "in the process of becoming":

1. How will we ever engage in critical self-examination or reflection as a means to better ensure "good teaching" than a standardized robotic curriculum ever could?
2. How will we have the capacity to see our students for who they are, who they wish to be, or who they might become?

Some of this might feel risky. As Bukowski (1975) reminds us in his poem *Style*, such creative efforts *are* "dangerous," and critical post avant-garde approaches to teaching, as a style for developing a left-handed curriculum, are a "way of doing . . . a way of being done . . . that makes all the difference" (n.p.).

Teachers need to take back their profession. Teachers need creativity in order to imagine a new narrative; to rewrite their *own* identities. There's a passage I read somewhere (sadly I can't remember exactly where to give credit where credit is due . . .), but basically it said that if you want to colonize a people, you first take away their capacity to make art. Why? Because it's through the creative imagination that we have the power to redefine for ourselves the world we wish to be in. If you wish to foster complacency and complicity in a group of people, remove their abilities to be creative.

It may seem a bit extreme to associate education reform with cultural genocide of a nation, but I think we'd be foolish to overlook some of the similarities. When the Europeans wanted the lands of Indigenous people in the "New World," what did they do first? In order to oppress a population you first have to justify your actions as morally sound, right? So the colonizers cast the indigenous people as lazy, stupid, unskilled, uneducated or "heathen," right? A people in need of . . . wait for it, folks. . . . "REFORM"!

Our public schools are one of the last American land grabs for profit. These are dangerous times. And they require a dangerous style—creative teaching. I'll give you one brief example: the Tucson, AZ Ethnic Studies program. Do you want to know the real reason why they shut that program down? Because . . . *it was working*. It was increasing the graduation rate. Students were learning. They were being successful. The teachers in that program embodied creative teaching as its finest hour. Dangerous style through creative teaching invites change you see. Creativity reminds teachers that they have the power to take risks, to do a dangerous thing with style, and offers the skill sets needed to resist this destruction of their profession.

It is by being *this* kind of role model that we can successfully practice these same principals in our classrooms. The lip service teachers get from policymakers trickles down to what teachers say to their students: "Be creative. Take a risk. But you better get it right on the test, *or else . . .*" It's a mixed message. If you have children (in a classroom, or your own at home, or even if you're a grandparent) you know that the old adage, "Do as I say, not as I do" does not work. It's not enough to just imagine other worlds and other possibilities—you have to believe you have the capabilities, the creative tools, to create them. And then you must take action. We must replace fear-based punitive measures used in schools all over this country with:

- Measures that put into place supports for teachers to *act creatively*.
- Curriculum that inspires students to *want* to learn.
- Practices that attach real meaningful practices and that foster a wide-awakeness in our children.

So ironically, the skills and capacities we most desperately need the most— creative thinking to face the challenges of a changing and complex world— are the same skills we are so quick to eliminate. We forgo art, music, and PE in favor of more test prep. We fire teachers and increase class size, while 45 billion dollars goes into the coffers of testing companies. What does that say about us as a society? We need to teach teachers how to be more creative, not how to be more compliant.

The creative elements outlined in this book are the foundations of a left-handed curriculum: Creativity for democracy, freedom, voice, empowerment, and ongoing hope for change when change is needed. None of this will come with an instruction manual. It's ours to write on the wall of daily experience.

You see, creativity and complacency cannot exist in the same space. Which do we want for our children and for ourselves? A world that is constructed for us by others, or one in which we give children the tools to make a world for themselves? What is our choice to be? We need creativity, not compliance, to reimagine and protect our public schools. And we need teachers—*great* teachers—to show us how it can be done.

If teachers are to take themselves out of the periphery and back into the center of what it means to develop and practice curriculum and to discover possible futures, then we can only do so through the lens of an artist. Bringing ourselves as conscious creators into the equation means cutting loose from the anchors of absolute knowledge and singular visions (especially those crafted by others for us.) This is necessary for us to say what otherwise can't be said, to draw out the essence of the meaning we seek from the cracks between the cement, and to seek (well-armed) the untold possibilities from out of the darkness.

8

Epilogue

> *Sometimes deviation from the usual is a special revelation of truth. In alchemy this was referred to as the opus contra naturam . . . When normality explodes or breaks out into craziness or shadow, we might look closely, before running for cover and before attempting to restore familiar order, at the potential meaningfulness of the event.*
>
> —Thomas Moore, in hooks, 1995, p. 17

So what can a left-handed curriculum when enacted in a classroom look like? During one of my Lesley courses, I told that teacher-cohort that as an "informal and ungraded homework assignment" that they should each find one thing to do that was subversive in their teaching. By subversive I did not mean "illegal," or anything *radical.* Simply, I suggested they perform an act that was outside the bounds of what they would normally do— something that would "subvert" the scripted expectations and demands of their regular curriculum. One teacher took this assignment to heart and held a "Subversive Day" in her classroom. The following is an essay she wrote describing what she did, why, and the outcome. Her efforts, as described here, are powerful representations of emergence, collaboration, and transformation in action. Within the open-ended and creative approach she took, one can see elements of curriculum as space, community, identity, composition, and empowerment-both for herself and her students. She called this the

"Not-Curriculum Experiment." This is just one of a myriad of possible ways that educators can empower themselves and transform their teaching and student learning. Just imagine if more classrooms could look like this:

As teachers, we would all like to think that we mold our lessons to incorporate rigor and meaningfulness in to everything we offer our students. Included in this however, we must not lose sight of choice, variety, novelty, and relevance. The charge from Dr. McDermott was to do something subversive! I loved the challenge, and took what I had already been doing and made it extreme. To show, or rather prove, that children, given the opportunity, will excel if given control over their learning environment and how they produce work, I cleared my classroom and gave my students choices over every part of their day.

I asked my class, "How do you learn best?" With Expo marker in hand, I started vigorously writing down all the answers that started flying my way. "I have to read it over and over," "I like games," "I need to hear it," "I do my work better when there is music or noise in the background," "I learn best from my mistakes," "When we use our slates," "I have to see it," "I like to work in partners," "I like to work in groups," "I like to work by myself," "Can we do something with food?"

My next question was, "What do you learn best in?" OK, this did really throw them. There were bubbles of "What is she getting at?" swarming over their little heads. One last question, "Would you choose a desk, or no desk?" My students were hooked. Then I dropped it on them, "On Friday we are going to have a day completely arranged around how you learn best—not just for one subject—but for the entire day. Not necessarily you as a group, but every single one of you, as an individual." I was committed to taking this space we call a classroom and transforming it. As the wheels began to turn, the questions started to unfold again. "Do we have to sit at our desk?" No. "So we can wear our pajamas?" Yes. "Do we have to wear our pajamas?" No. "Can we wear like our athletic stuff?" Yes. "Can I wear my funny shirt?" Yes. Finally I said, "People, you can wear whatever you want as long as it covers your body and is appropriate!" My thought, why are today's children so rigid and conformed already? They have to have a ten minute discussion just to clarify clothing. Why is it so radical to think of their square room in a different way?

Somehow, in the light of the question, "How do you learn best?" they had a difficult time equating the two. Why do we impose restrictions on our kids? This was my opportunity show that it was OK to follow and honor their will. That Friday, the kids molded their day, chose what they wanted to wear, decided if they wanted to work at a desk or not, and produced what *I* wanted, the way *they* wanted. It worked.

After plodding through closet suggestions, I asked "Who wants a desk?" Four people wanted a desk, the rest did not. So, four people got desks, and the rest of the desks were banned from my room and banished to the hall (which drew a lot of questions and interest from kids and teachers alike). They were replaced with blankets. The next day or so was very revealing for me as a teacher. I drew out "groups," tried to plan lessons, wrote, erased, thought, rethought. What am I going to do to hit every single thing the kids had listed off? And then it occurred to me why I was doing this in the first place—to give them choice, to let them choose the method, to let them organize their learning and thinking. Why was I working and fretting so much, why was I falling back into the old way of planning every minute of their day, why have *I* not let go? On Thursday, I let them know what I was thinking, or not thinking, and asked them what they thought about my . . . nonthoughts.

Another radical question by Mrs. C, "There are some things I need from you tomorrow, all I need to know is how you want to give them to me and what I need to provide for you." I need story elements, somehow, some way, what do you need from me to make that happen? I need fractions, somehow, some way. I need grammar, somehow, some way. Lastly, something that I knew they would enjoy a debate for social studies: Loyalists vs. Patriots. Ready, go! Story elements turned in to a book of their choice, one they were already reading, had read, or would read during class, and several bins of "stuff." There was construction paper, paint and brushes, markers, crayons and pencils, glue and tape, paper plates, pipe cleaners, play dough, clay, yarn, Legos, craft sticks, and straws . . . really, anything they could find. Now that I filled their story element request, it was time for math. They requested the laptops for ixl.com—a fabulous program that they love and beg to work on. Also requested were marshmallows, toothpicks, and pancakes. Done. How about grammar, not exactly the most favorite thing to do among any set of children. I had one hand go up—"Can we make our own *Mad Libs?*" There was a resounding cheer and affirmation . . . so it shall be! I let them know about our debate and they were all over that. I have a rather opinionated and competitive class (16 boys, 9 girls) so that was a no brainer. Now all we needed was execution day.

I was sitting at my desk as they all came trickling in. The first, who came wearing his pajamas, got the "best spot" (the best . . . for him), under the table he went. It was like he went into a cave. This five-foot boy meticulously arranged his blanket and books under our long table in the back of the room. The next child that came in, wearing his "funny shirt," spread his camouflaged blanket right smack in the middle of the floor—he was on an island! Slowly but surely the room filled and there was a floor of fluff. My four desks were filled as well. They all housed boys wearing "regular" clothes...jeans and a shirt. I love it! I'm not sure what *it* is, but it is big, and I love it.

After morning announcements, lunch count, and attendance, the first lesson of the day was issued: "I need to know that you know the elements of a story." I showed them what was around the room to use, told them I trusted them to move and get their supplies in a polite manner, and then I let them go. They read, created, read more, created more, and sometimes changed what they were creating. Some of them made games, some made play dough sculptures, some drew, some just used pencil and paper, and some painted their story elements.

What was the result? Total engagement, total rigor, and total relevance! For the first time in the history of this particular class, they were completely quiet for over an hour! They read, created, read more, created more, and sometimes changed what they were creating. Some of them made games, some made play dough sculptures, some drew, some just used pencil and paper, and some painted. Interestingly, a few produced work—exactly like we have done in class before—no deviation, simply drawing on what they had already been "manufactured" to do. They were not the ones that were in the desks either, and it was a mix of boys and girls. Regardless, all the children were busy doing what they wanted to do while producing and intertwining with the knowledge that I needed from them.

During reading, half of the time I had music on, half of the time it was off—just to switch it up a bit. All of my kids like the music on—I tend to think it is the type of music I play—unknown to them, no lyrics, and unpredictable in their minds. It breaks up the sometimes stale institutional silence of the classroom. As we slipped into math, I got out my griddle.

We had been studying Tall Tales that same week which definitely called for some Paul Bunyan pancakes to tie in the food request. The wafting odor of pancakes and syrup filled the air like Saturday morning breakfast at home. Was this a better learning environment for some? I know our school counselor benefited. When she came in the room to relay some information I offered her some—she had not had breakfast, so they were a welcomed treat! She gushed at what was going on in the room—is our learning environment now starting to trickle out to the rest of the school? We'll see. For the time being, it was all about laptops, fractions, and pancakes! After lunch, which of course we brought back to our room to eat per the kids, and after recess, the rest of the day was devoted to the debate and to the creation of our *Mad Libs.*

The bell rang, the day ended, the kids went home, and I thought, "Wow, it actually worked." I went home exhausted and content. Content in knowing I did what was best for them, exhausted from being anxious from the thinking all day... did I actually do what was best for them? I colored outside the line, I didn't stick to what the "authorities" in my teacher editions said to do, I did what my kids wanted to do, and not what I thought they should do based on what they need to know to become a successful CEO.

References

Anderson, G., & Herr, K. (2007). *Encyclopedia of activism and social justice.* Newbury Park, CA: Sage Publications.

Anderson, T. (2011). An introduction to Art education for social justice. In T. Anderson, D. Gussak, K. K. Hallmark, and A. Paul (Eds.) *Art education for social justice* (pp. 2–13). Reston, VA: National Art Education Association.

Apple, M. (2000). "Hey man, I'm good": The aesthetics and ethics of making films in schools. In G. Willis & W. Schubert (Eds.), *Reflections from the heart of educational inquiry: Understanding curriculum and teaching through the arts* (pp. 213–221). Troy, NY: Educators International Press.

Applebaum, A. (2000). Performed by the space: The spatial turn. *Journal of Curriculum Theorizing, 16*(3), 35–53.

Au, W. (2011). Teaching in dystopia. In W. Au & M. Tempel (Eds.), *Pencil down: Rethinking high-stakes testing and accountability in public schools* (pp. 73–77). Milwaukee, WI: Rethinking Schools.

Ayers, W. (2004). *Teaching toward freedom.* Boston MA: Beacon Press.

Barone, T. (2000). *Aesthetics, politics, and educational inquiry: Essays and examples.* New York, NY: Peter Lang.

Beattie, M. (2001). *The art of learning to teach: Pre-service teacher narratives.* Upper Saddle River, NJ: Merrill Prentice Hall.

Bender, L. (Producer), & Tarantino, Q. (Director). (1994). *Pulp fiction* [Motion picture]. Los Angeles CA: Mirimax Films.

Berger, J. (1993). *Sense of sight.* (Vintage International Ed edition) New York, NY: Vintage. [Originally published as *The White bird* (1985). London, UK: Chatto and Windus]

Beyer, L. (2000). The arts and education: Personal agency and social possibility. In G. Willis & W. Schubert (Eds.), *Reflections from the heart of educational in-*

The Left Handed Curriculum, pages 129–136
Copyright © 2013 by Information Age Publishing

quiry: Understanding curriculum and teaching through the arts (pp. 197–204). Troy, NY: Educators International Press.

Block, A. (1998). Curriculum as affichiste: Popular culture and identity. In W. Pinar (Ed.), *Curriculum: Toward new identities* (pp. 325–341). New York, NY: Garland Publishing.

Boal, A. (2002). *Games for actors and non actors* (2nd ed.). New York, NY: Routledge.

Boggs, G. L., & Kurashige, S. (2011). *The next American Revolution: Sustainable activism for the twenty-first century*. Berkeley, CA: University of California Press.

Bonami, F. (Ed). (1996). *In echoes: Contemporary art at the age of endless conclusions*. New York, NY: The Montacelli Press.

Bowers, C. A. (1995). *Educating for an ecologically sustainable culture: Rethinking moral education, creativity, intelligence, and other modern orthodoxies*. New York, NY: SUNY Press.

Brown v. Board of Education of Topeka (347 U.S. 483). Retrieved from http://www.nationalcenter.org/brown.html

Bukowski, C. (1975). *Style*. On *Poems and insults* [Audio recording]. San Francisco, CA: Bitter Lemon Records.

Burdick, J., Sandlin, J. A., & O'Malley, M. P. (Eds.). (in press). *Problematizing public pedagogy*. New York, NY: Routledge.

Cardoso, W. (2011). The hidden curriculum of space. Retrieved from http://authenticteaching.wordpress.com/2011/03/29/the-hidden-curriculum-of-space/

Carey, R. (1998). *Critical art pedagogy: Foundations for a postmodern art education*. New York, NY: Garland.

Carpenter, S., & Springgay, S. (2011). Editor's introduction: The politics of creativity, urban renewal, and education. *Journal of Curriculum and Pedagogy, 8*(2), 97–100.

Castillo, G. (1974). *Left-handed teaching: Lessons in affective education*. New York, NY: Praeger Publishers.

Chilcott, L. (Producer), & Guggeheim, D. (Director). (2010). *Waiting for Superman* [Motion picture]. United States: Paramount Pictures.

Churchill, J. (2010). Retrieved from http://blog.pbk.org/

Clandinin, J., & Connelly, M. (2000). Narrative Inquiry: Experience and story in qualitative research. San Francisco, CA: Jossey-Bass.

Copperthwaite, W. M. S. (2007). *A Handmade life: In search of simplicity*. White River Junction, VT: Chelsea Green Publishing.

Cornelius, C. (1999). *Iroquois corn in a culture-based curriculum*. Albany, NY: SUNY Press.

Davis, D., & Butler-Kisber, L. (1999). *Arts-based representation in qualitative research: Collage as a contextualizing strategy*. Paper presented at AERA Annual Meeting, Montreal, Quebec, April, 1999.

Desai, D. (2009). Imagining justice in times of perpetual war: Notes from the classroom. *Journal of Curriculum and Pedagogy, (6)*2, 6–25.

Dewey J. (1997). *Democracy and education.* New York, NY: Free Press. (Original work published in 1916)

Diamond, C. T. P., & Mullen, C. A. (1999). *The postmodern educator: Arts-based inquiries and teacher development.* New York, NY: Peter Lang.

Dixon, M. B., & Smith, J. A. (1995). *Anne Bogart: Viewpoints.* Lyme, NH: Smith and Kraus.

Facebook. Out of the Box Doll Project. https://www.facebook.com/pages/Out-of-the-Box-Doll-Project/219816944721693?ref=hl

de Freitas, E. (2011). Parkour and the built environment: Spatial practices and the plasticity of school buildings. *Journal of Curriculum Theorizing, 27*(3), 209–220.

Folk Tree. (n.d.). *Jorge Rosano: The art of Mexican paper cutting.* Retrieved from www.folktree.com

Freire, P. (1998). *Pedagogy of freedom: Ethics, democracy, and civic courage.* Oxford, UK: Rowan and Littlefield Publishers.

Freire, P. (2000). *Pedagogy of the oppressed.* New York, NY: Continuum Press. (Original work published in 1970)

Foucault, M. (1979). *Discipline and punish: The birth of the prison.* New York, NY: Random House.

Gablik, S. (1991). *The re-enchantment of art.* New York, NY: Thames & Hudson.

Gablik, S. (1997). *Conversations before the end of time.* New York, NY: Thames & Hudson.

Gardner, H. (1999). *Intelligence reframed: Multiple intelligences for the 21st century.* New York, NY: Basic Books.

Gatzambide-Fernandez, R. (2010). Toward creative solidarity in the next "moment" of curriculum work. In E. Malewski (Ed.), *Curriculum studies handbook: The next moment* (pp. 78–93). New York, NY: Taylor and Francis.

Gaztambide-Fernandez, R. (2004). Introduction, in R. Gaztambide-Fernandez & J.T. Sears (Eds.), *Curriculum work as a public moral enterprise* (p vii–xvii). Lanham, MD: Rowman and Littlefield Publishers.

Gazetas, A. (2003). A cultural politics, film narratives, and adult education: Changing identities in a postmodern world. In E. Hasebe-Ludt & W. Hurren (Eds.), *Curriculum intertext: Place/language/pedagogy* (pp. 189–202). New York, NY: Peter Lang.

Gilbert, I., & Ryan, W. (2011). *Inspirational Teachers Inspirational Learners: A book of hope for creativity and the curriculum in the twenty first century.* New York, NY: Crown House Publishing.

Goldbard, A. (2006). *The new creative community: The art of cultural development.* Oakland, CA: New Village Press.

Goldstone, J., Forstater, M, & White, M. (Producers), & Gilliam, T., & Jones, T. (Directors). (1974). *Monty Python and the Holy Grail* [Motion picture]. Great Britain: Python (Monty) Pictures LTD.

Green, R. (Writer), & Thompson, R. (Director). (1992). Burning down the house [*Television series episode*] In D. Chase, A. Schneider, & D. Frolov (Producers), *Northern exposure.* Los Angeles, CA: CBS Network.

Greene, M. (1995). *Releasing the imagination: Essays on education, the arts, and social change.* San Francisco, CA: Jossey-Bass.

Griffiths, J. (2004). *A sideways look at time.* New York, NY: Tarcher.

Grumet, M. (1978). Songs and situations: The figure/ground relation in a case study of Currere. In G. Willis (Ed.) *Qualitiative Inquiry* (pp. 276–315). Berkley, CA: McCutchan Publishing.

Grumet, M. (1993). The play of meanings in the art of teaching. *Theory into Practice, 32*(4), 204–209.

Grumet, M. (2000). Curriculum and the art of daily life. In G. Willis & W. Schubert (Eds.), *Reflections from the heart of educational inquiry: Understanding curriculum and teaching through the arts* (pp. 74–90). Troy, NY: Educators International Press.

hooks, b. (1995). *Art on my mind: Visual politics.* New York, NY: The New Press.

jagodinski, j. (1992). Curriculum as felt through six layers of an aesthetically embodied skin: The arch writing on the body. In W. Pinar & W. Reynolds (Eds.), *Understanding curriculum as phenomenological and deconstructed text* (pp. 159–183). New York, NY: Teachers College Press.

jagodinski, j. (1997). *Pun(k) deconstruction: Experifigural writing in art and art education.* Mahwah, NJ: Lawrence Erlbaum Associates.

Jardine, W., Graham, T., LaGrange, A., & Kisling-Saunders, H. (2006). "Staying within the lines": Re-imagining what is "elementary" in the art of schooling. In D. Jardine, S. Friesen, & P. Clifford (Eds.), *Curriculum in abundance* (pp. 214–227). Mahwah, NJ: Lawrence Erlbaum Associates.

Jungle Brothers. (1989). Acknowledge your own history [Lyrics by Mike G]. On *Done by the Forces of Nature* [Audio recording]. Los Angeles, CA: Warner Studios.

Landsman, J. (2011). Wherefore art? *Journal of Curriculum and Pedagogy 8*(2), 127–130.

Levy, S. (1996). *Starting from scratch.* Portsmouth, NH: Heinemann.

Lubart, T. I. (2000). Models of the creative process: past, present and future. *Creativity Research Journal, 13*(3/4), 295–303.

Luse, M. (2010). A look at art and public pedagogy in New York City. Retrieved from http://www.indypendent.org/2010/06/02/essay-look-art-and-public-pedagogy-new-york-city

Marks, H., & Louis, K. (1999). Teacher empowerment and the capacity for organizational learning. *Education Administration Quarterly, 35*(5), 707–750.

Massey, D. B. (1995). *Spatial divisions of labor: Social structures and the geography of production* (2nd ed.). New York, NY: Routledge.

May, W. (2000). The arts and curriculum as lingering. In G. Willis & W. Schubert (Eds.), *Reflections from the heart of educational inquiry: Understanding curriculum and teaching through the arts* (pp. 140–152). Troy, NY: Educators International Press.

McDermott, M. (2001). *Flinging the piano of critical post avant-garde arts based inquiry.* (Doctoral dissertation). University of Virginia, Charlottesville, VA.

McDermott, M. (2003). Collaging pre-service teacher identity in critical post avant-garde inquiry. *Teacher Education Quarterly: Arts-Based Research in Teacher Education, 29*(4), 53–68.

McDermott, M. (2004). It's not the thing you fling: Exploring democracy in education through post avant-garde art. *Democracy and Education: Teaching the arts for social justice (Special Issue), 15*(3), 23–31.

McDermott, M. (2005). Torn to pieces: Emergence, collaboration, and transformation in pre-service teacher education. In M. C. Powell & V. Marcow-Speiser (Eds.), *The arts, education, and social change: Little signs of hope* (pp. 10–19). New York, NY: Peter Lang.

McDermott, M (2011). Curriculum of the eye/I. *Journal of Curriculum and Pedagogy, 27*(2), 130–144.

McDermott, M., & Daspit, T. (1999, October). Opus (alchemical), contra (correspon…) naturam (…dences): Infusions, transfusions, and reve(a)lations in curriculum theorizing. Paper presented at *The Curriculum Theorizing Conference on Curriculum Theory and Classroom Practice*, Dayton, OH.

McDermott, M., Daspit, T., & Dodd, K. (2003). Using theater as pedagogy: Implications of dramatic approaches for democratic dialogue. In R. Gaztambide-Fernandez & J. T. Sears (Eds.), *Curriculum work as public moral enterprise* (pp. 24–31). Lanham, MD: Rowman and Littlefield.

McLaren, P. (1998). *Life in schools : an introduction to critical pedagogy in the foundations of education* (3rd ed.). New York, NY: Longman

McNeill, M. (2011). *Duncan meets with 'Save Our Schools' organizers, and their dolls.* Retrieved from http://blogs.edweek.org/edweek/campaign-k12/2011/07/duncan_meets_with_school_march.html

McNiff, S. (1992). *Art as medicine.* Boston, MA: Shambala Publications.

Miller, P. (2003). Retrieved from http://fusionanomaly.net/djspooky.html

Molyneaux, B. L. (Ed.) (1997). *The cultural life of images.* New York, NY: Routledge.

Mullen, C. (1999). Whiteness, cracks, and ink stains: Making cultural identity with Euroamerican pre-service teachers. In C. T. P. Diamond & C. A. Mullen (Eds.), *The postmodern educator: Arts-based inquiries and teacher development* (pp. 147–185). New York, NY: Peter Lang.

Nachmanovitch, S. (1990). *Free play: Improvisation in life and art.* New York, NY: Tarcher Publishing.

A Nation at Risk. (1983). U.S. Department of Education's National Commission on Excellence in Education published report.

O'Malley, M. P. (2006). *Public moral leadership and dissent from a standardization of human experience.* Paper presented at the Annual Meeting of the Curriculum and Pedagogy Group. Balcones Springs, Texas.

Overlie, M. (n.d.). Retrieved from http://www.sixviewpoints.com/Theory_1.html

OWP Architects, VS Furniture, & Bruce Mau Designs (2010). *The third teacher: 79 ways you can use design to transform teaching & learning.* New York, NY: Abrams.

Paley, N. (1995). *Finding arts place.* New York, NY: Routledge.

Pinar, W. (1998). *Curriculum: Towards new identities.* New York, NY: Garland Press.

Pinar, W. (2000). The white cockatoo: images of abstract expressionism in curriculum theory. In G. Willis & W. Schubert (Eds.), *Reflections from the heart of educational inquiry:* Understanding curriculum and teaching through the arts (pp. 244–250). Troy, NY: Educators International Press.

Pinar, W., & Grumet, M. (1978). *Toward a poor curriculum.* Dubuque, IA: Hunt Publishing Company.

Pinar, W., Reynolds, W., Slattery, P., & Taubman, P. (1995). *Understanding curriculum.* New York, NY: Peter Lang.

Powell, M. C., & Speiser, V. (2004). *Arts, education, and social change: Little signs of hope.* New York, NY: Peter Lang Publishers.

Prown, J. D. (1982). Mind in matter. *Winterhur Portfolio, 14*(1), 253–269.

Raffi, C. (2010). Quote in OWP/P Architects, VS Furniture and Bruce Mau Design (Eds.), *The third teacher: 79 Ways you can use design to transform teaching and learning* (p. 32). New York, NY: Abrams Books.

Reinsborough, P., & Cannine, D. (2010). *Re:claiming change: How to use story-based strategy to win campaigns, build movements and change the world.* Oakland, CA: PM Press.

Rethorst, J. (1997). Art and the imagination: Cognitive science for moral education. *Philosophy of Education,* 278–284. Retrieved from http://ojs.ed.uiuc.edu/index.php/pes/article/view/2205/900

Rice, E. M., & Schneider, G. (1994). Decade of teacher empowerment: An empirical analysis of teacher involvement in decision making, 1980–1991. *Journal of Educational Administration, 32*(1), 43–58.

Richards, M. C., & Haynes, D. (1996). *Opening our moral eye: Essays, talks & poems embracing creativity and community.* Aurora, CO: Lindisfarne Press.

Robinson, K. (2006). *Do schools kill creativity?* Retrieved from http://www.ted.com/talks/ken_robinson_says_schools_kill_creativity.html

Robinson, P., & Lewis, C. (2011). The troubling context of urban schools: Instructional design as a source of transformation for students of color. *Journal of Curriculum and Pedagogy, 8*(2), 109–112.

Saltmarsh, J. (2007). *Introduction to Wm. S. Coperthwaite's A handmade life: In search of simplicity* (pp. 1–6). White River Junction, VT: Chelsea Green Publishing.

Sandlin, J., O'Mally, M., & Burdick, J. (2011). Mapping the complexity of public pedagogy scholarship 1894–2010. *Review of Educational Research, 81*(3), 338–375.

Sandlin, S., Kahn, R., Darts, D., & Tavin, K. (2009). To find the cost of freedom: Theorizing and practicing a critical pedagogy of consumption. *Journal for Critical Education Policy Studies, 7*(2), 99–125.

Schwarzman, M., & Knight, K. (2005). *Beginner's guide to community-based arts.* New York, NY: New Village Press.

Slattery, P. (1999). Popular culture and higher education: Using aesthetics and seminars to reconceptualize curriculum. In T. Daspit & J. Weaver (Eds.), *Popular culture and critical pedagogy* (pp. 33–49). New York, NY: Garland.

Slattery, P., Krasney, K., & O'Mally, M. (2007). Hermeneutics, aesthetics, and the quest for answerability: A dialogic possibility for reconceptualizing the interpretive processing curriculum studies. *Journal of Curriculum Studies, 39*(5), 537–558.

Spencer, H. (1861). *Education: Intellectual, moral and physical.* London, UK: Williams and Norgate. [Reprinted in 1932 with an Introduction by F. A. Cavenagh]. Cambridge, UK: Cambridge University Press.

Springgay, S. (2004). Inside the invisible: Arts-based educational research as excess. *Journal of Curriculum and Pedagogy, 1*(1), 8–18.

Starko, A. (2010). *Creativity in the classroom: Schools of curious delight.* New York, NY: Routledge.

Sternberg, R.J., & Lubart, T. (1996). Investing in creativity. *American Psychologist, 51*(7), 677–688.

Sumara, L., & Davis, B. (1998). Underpainting. *Journal of Curriculum Theorizing, 14*(4), 1–5.

Taffee, S. (2009). Constraining innovation: Teacher-proof curricula. Retrieved from http://taffee.edublogs.org/2009/05/17/constraining-innovation-teacher-proof-curricula/

Tan, A. (2007). *Creativity: A handbook for teachers.* Singapore: World Scientific Publishing Company.

Tan, A., & Lai-Chong, L. (2004). *Creativity for teachers.* Singapore: Marshall Cavendish Academic Press.

Thunfors, J. (2007). *Journalist without words: 19 years painting international conversations.* Southport, CT: Riverside Publishing.

Thunfors, J. (2009). *Paint your life.* Southport, CT: Riverside.

Tierney, W. G., & Lincoln, Y. S. (1997). Introduction: Explorations and discoveries. In W. G. Tierney & Y. S. Lincoln (Eds.), *Representation and the text: Re-framing the narrative voice* (vii–2). Albany, NY: SUNY Press.

Turner, J. (2010). Teaching is a political act. *Teacher News Magazine, 23*(2). Retrieved from http://www.bctf.ca/publications/NewsmagArticle.aspx?id=21678)

Tyler, R. W. (1949). *Basic principles of curriculum and instruction.* Chicago, IL: The University of Chicago Press.

Weida, C. L. (2011). Revisiting/revising art and home: (Be)longing and identity in out-of-school art education setting. *Teaching Artist Journal, 9*(3), 145–155.

Willinsky, J. (2006). How to be more of a public intellectual by making your intellectual work more public. *Journal of Curriculum and Pedagogy, 3*(1) 92–95.

Willis, G. (1978). *Qualitative evaluation.* Berkley, CA: McCutcheon Publishing Corporation.

Willis, G., & Schubert, W. (Eds.). (2000). *Reflections from the heart of educational inquiry: Understanding curriculum and teaching through the arts.* Troy, NY: Educators International Press.

Wilson, E. (2000). Learning concepts. In P. Warwick & R. S. Linfield (Eds.) *Science 3-13: The past, the present and possible futures* (pp. 37–48). London, UK: RoutledgeFalmer.

Wolf, N. (2007). *End of America: Letters of warning to a young patriot.* New York, NY: Chelsea Publishers.

About the Author

Dr. **Morna McDermott** is an Associate Professor at Towson University, where she teaches various theory and methods courses in the College of Education. Her scholarship and research interests focus on democracy, social justice, and arts-informed inquiry in K–post secondary educational settings, and working with beginning and experienced educators. She explores how the arts serve as a form of literacy that challenges traditional classroom learning and dominant narratives. She currently lives in Baltimore with her husband and two children.

Lightning Source UK Ltd.
Milton Keynes UK
UKOW06f1101150816

280718UK00001B/134/P